"If I could go back and pick one book to prepare for the onslaught of ministerial challenges our church has faced this year, it would be this one. Weary pastors, discouraged deacons, and churches struggling to stay on mission, get this book! It hits all the right notes."

Bobby Scott, Copastor, Community of Faith Bible Church, South Gate, California

"The church has long needed this decidedly biblical, highly readable, and very practical book. Grounding the diaconate in the person and work of Jesus, Matt Smethurst answers the multitude of contemporary questions with judiciousness and care, drawing upon his deep knowledge of Scripture, history, and church life. *Deacons* should long remain the standard text in both the local church and the academy."

Malcolm B. Yarnell III, Research Professor of Theology, Southwestern Baptist Theological Seminary; Teaching Pastor, Lakeside Baptist Church, Granbury, Texas

"My deepest concern in books on church polity is that the author would make his case based on solid Bible exposition, not denominational tradition or personal opinion. Smethurst has done this well: he has expounded the relevant texts on this widely misunderstood church office. With clear structure and striking insight, he recaptures the Bible's intention for deacons."

Alexander Strauch, author, *Biblical Eldership* and *Paul's Vision for the Deacons*

"There have been many helpful books on almost every area of church life, ministry, and polity. The one missing area has been a full-length book addressing deacons. This book fills that gap. Smethurst doesn't just explain the biblical teaching; he fleshes it out with numerous practical examples and illustrations."

John S. Hammett, Professor of Systematic Theology, Southeastern Baptist Theological Seminary; author, *Biblical Foundations for Baptist Churches*

"A wonderful resource on a neglected subject. It is biblical, accessible, and practical—ideal for those in the process of serving as a deacon. Indeed, deacons who assist the elders, organize service, care for the needy, preserve unity, and mobilize ministry are wonderful gifts to Christ's body. Smethurst explains and applies these ideas clearly, concisely, and compellingly."

Tony Merida, Lead Pastor, Imago Dei Church, Raleigh, North Carolina; author, *Ordinary*

"The church needs gospel-centered, theologically minded, servant-hearted deacons who care for others out of a deep love for Jesus. Smethurst offers historical context, biblical insight, and practical examples of this vital role in congregational life."

Melissa B. Kruger, Director of Women's Initiatives, The Gospel Coalition; author, *Growing Together*

"Considerable confusion surrounds diaconal ministry. Faithful deacons, Smethurst reminds us, protect the ministry of the Word, promote the unity of the body, and provide for the tangible needs of our most vulnerable members. I plan to buy multiple copies, regularly give them out to our congregation, and use the book to equip new deacons and encourage current ones."

Juan R. Sanchez, Senior Pastor, High Pointe Baptist Church, Austin, Texas; author, *The Leadership Formula*

"This book is accessible, engaging, and substantial. Both nonspecialists and readers with theological training will learn from its biblical, historical, and practical reflections on the diaconate, even where they may disagree with some of its conclusions. All readers should emerge from this book with zeal and appreciation for Christ's great gift of diaconal ministry."

Guy Prentiss Waters, Professor of New Testament, Reformed Theological Seminary, Jackson; author, *How Jesus Runs the Church*

"In some churches the office of deacon is underrated; members don't profit from deacons as they ought. In other churches the office is overrated; deacons want to function like and challenge the elders. Smethurst shows us the balanced and biblical view."

Conrad Mbewe, Pastor, Kabwata Baptist Church, Lusaka, Zambia

"Matt Smethurst serves churches well with this succinct treatment of deacons that is biblically faithful, pastorally relevant, and exceptionally clear. Even if you disagree with him (and you probably shouldn't), you will appreciate the tone in which he describes and defends the vital ministry of deacons. The feeling you get after reading this book is like being in a crowded theater that erupts with applause after a memorable movie."

Benjamin L. Merkle, Professor of New Testament and Greek, Southeastern Baptist Theological Seminary; author, *40 Questions about Elders and Deacons*

"Matt Smethurst showcases how essential deacons are to gospel ministry, even while debunking misconceptions and unhelpful traditions. Practical, beautifully written, and full of encouraging stories, this is a helpful guide to an essential office."

Jenny Manley, pastor's wife, United Arab Emirates; author, *The Good Portion: Christ*

"Smethurst's concise manifesto and practical manual succeeds in highlighting the glory of the office of deacon. This is not a dry, theoretical treatise but a clear and cogent call to recognize God's irreplaceable gift of the diaconal ministry."

Cornelis Van Dam, Emeritus Professor of Old Testament, Canadian Reformed Theological Seminary; author, *The Deacon*

"Matt Smethurst addresses a much neglected but vital part of church life. *Deacons* will encourage leaders and church members alike. It is full of biblical insight and inspiration. I can't recommend it too highly."

Sam Allberry, pastor; author, *7 Myths about Singleness*

"There is no greater joy in life than serving the Lord. What a unique calling it is to serve as a deacon. Smethurst will lead you in a process of loving God's highest calling: to be a servant. This book will help many!"

Johnny Hunt, Former President, Southern Baptist Convention; author, *The Deacon I Want to Be*

"Deacons have been the object of jokes for years—or worse, ignored. I love how Smethurst creatively fleshes out both the historical and biblical context of this important ministry—then presses into practical application. Use this crucial book to embrace and equip those called by God to serve as deacons."

Mark Dance, Former Executive Editor, *Deacon Magazine*

"It is uncommon to find great, biblical, clear, and insightful content packaged in a small book. This is one of those occurrences. Today's church needs this teaching urgently."

Miguel Núñez, Senior Pastor, Iglesia Bautista Internacional, Santo Domingo, Dominican Republic

"Dear reader, this is an excellent book! It is more interesting and important than you probably assume. You think I just have to say this because this is a blurb? Take a moment, open to chapter 1, and read the first page—just the first page!—then come back to this blurb. There are *lots* of other pages that good! You should buy the book now and read it. Go on and get some more copies, and get people studying it at your church. They will be encouraged and your church will be helped to flourish!"

Mark Dever, Pastor, Capitol Hill Baptist Church, Washington, DC

DEACONS

9Marks: Building Healthy Churches

Edited by Mark Dever and Jonathan Leeman

Deacons: How They Serve and Strengthen the Church, Matt Smethurst (2021)

Corporate Worship: How the Church Gathers as God's People, Matt Merker (2021)

Prayer: How Praying Together Shapes the Church, John Onwuchekwa (2018)

Biblical Theology: How the Church Faithfully Teaches the Gospel, Nick Roark and Robert Cline (2018)

Missions: How the Local Church Goes Global, Andy Johnson (2017)

Conversion: How God Creates a People, Michael Lawrence (2017)

Discipling: How to Help Others Follow Jesus, Mark Dever (2016)

The Gospel: How the Church Portrays the Beauty of Christ, Ray Ortlund (2014)

Expositional Preaching: How We Speak God's Word Today, David R. Helm (2014)

Evangelism: How the Whole Church Speaks of Jesus, J. Mack Stiles (2014)

Church Elders: How to Shepherd God's People Like Jesus, Jeramie Rinne (2014)

Sound Doctrine: How a Church Grows in the Love and Holiness of God, Bobby Jamieson (2013)

Church Membership: How the World Knows Who Represents Jesus, Jonathan Leeman (2012)

Church Discipline: How the Church Protects the Name of Jesus, Jonathan Leeman (2012)

BUILDING HEALTHY CHURCHES

DEACONS

HOW THEY
SERVE
AND
STRENGTHEN
THE CHURCH

MATT SMETHURST

CROSSWAY®

WHEATON, ILLINOIS

Deacons: How They Serve and Strengthen the Church

Copyright © 2021 by Matt Smethurst

Published by Crossway
1300 Crescent Street
Wheaton, Illinois 60187

Cover illustration: Wayne Brezinka

First printing 2021

Printed in the United States of America

Hardcover ISBN: 978-1-4335-7162-6
ePub ISBN: 978-1-4335-7165-7
PDF ISBN: 978-1-4335-7163-3
Mobipocket ISBN: 978-1-4335-7164-0

Library of Congress Cataloging-in-Publication Data

Names: Smethurst, Matt, author.
Title: Deacons : how they serve and strengthen the church / Matt Smethurst.
Description: Wheaton, Illinois : Crossway, [2021] | Series: 9Marks: build-
   ing healthy churches | Includes bibliographical references and index.
Identifiers: LCCN 2020027561 (print) | LCCN 2020027562
   (ebook) | ISBN
9781433571626 (hardcover) | ISBN 9781433571633 (pdf) | ISBN
   9781433571640 (mobi) | ISBN 9781433571657 (epub)
Subjects: LCSH: Deacons.
Classification: LCC BV680 .S58 2021 (print) | LCC BV680 (ebook) | DDC
262/.14—dc23
LC record available at https://lccn.loc.gov/2020027561
LC ebook record available at https://lccn.loc.gov/2020027562

Crossway is a publishing ministry of Good News Publishers.

LB		31	30	29	28	27	26	25	24	23	22
15	14	13	12	11	10	9	8	7	6	5	4	3

To my parents, Doug and Lynda,
for modeling Christlike service my entire life.
I love you.

CONTENTS

SERIES PREFACE

Do you believe it's your responsibility to help build a healthy church? If you are a Christian, we believe that it is.

Jesus commands you to make disciples (Matt. 28:18–20). Jude says to build yourselves up in the faith (Jude 20–21). Peter calls you to use your gifts to serve others (1 Pet. 4:10). Paul tells you to speak the truth in love so that your church will become mature (Eph. 4:13, 15). Do you see where we are getting this?

Whether you are a church member or leader, the Building Healthy Churches series of books aims to help you fulfill such biblical commands and so play your part in building a healthy church. Another way to say it might be, we hope these books will help you grow in loving your church like Jesus loves your church.

In this series, 9Marks has produced short, readable books on each of what Mark has called nine marks of a healthy church—plus a few more. These include books on expositional preaching, biblical theology, sound doctrine, the gospel, conversion, evangelism, church membership, church discipline, discipleship and growth, church elders, deacons, prayer, missions, and corporate worship.

Local churches exist to display God's glory to the nations. We do that by fixing our eyes on the gospel of Jesus Christ, trusting him for salvation, and then loving one another with God's own holiness, unity, and love. We pray the book you are holding will help.

With hope,
Mark Dever and Jonathan Leeman
series editors

INTRODUCTION

"At Your Service"

I wonder why you opened this book (besides the arresting title that caught your attention). I can envision various scenarios.

1. *You're a pastor.*

   - You're an aspiring pastor who wants to study deacons.
   - You're a new pastor who wants to implement deacons.
   - You're a seasoned pastor who wants to rethink or redeploy deacons.
   - You're a frustrated pastor who wants to fire deacons.

2. *You're a deacon.*

   - You're a potential deacon who wants to understand the role.
   - You're a new deacon who wants to adjust to the role.
   - You're a seasoned deacon who wants to grow in the role.
   - You're a frustrated deacon who wants to quit the role.

3. *You're a church member.*

   - You like how deacons function in your church—and you're curious to learn more.

- You don't like how deacons function in your church—and you're curious if there's a better way.
- You simply desire to better grasp Scripture's teaching on this topic.

Or perhaps you've got another reason altogether. Suffice it to say, the topic of deacons—even just the *word*—can spark vastly different feelings among Christians. For some, the word is a bit nostalgic, perhaps a throwback to their childhood church. For others, it's beautiful; the word brings beloved faces to mind—specific servants laboring for the welfare of Christ's church. Yet for too many it's a painful word. It's painful for many *pastors*. How many times has the work of a church been hindered and harmed by those called to be its most exemplary servants?

EVERYONE DEACONS

If you've put your trust in Christ, you are already a deacon in a broad sense. The Greek noun *diakonos* appears twenty-nine times in the New Testament and is almost always translated "servant(s)"[1] or "minister(s)."[2] (Same with the related noun[3] and verb.[4]) Here are a few examples from the Gospels, rendered literally:

[1] Matt. 20:26; 23:11; Mark 9:35; 10:43; John 2:5, 9; 12:26; Rom. 13:4; 15:8; 1 Cor. 3:5; 2 Cor. 6:4; 11:15, 23; Eph. 3:7; 6:21; Col. 4:7; 1 Tim. 4:6.
[2] 2 Cor. 3:6; Col. 1:7, 23, 25.
[3] The noun *diakonia* is used thirty-four times to describe "ministry(ies)" (Acts 1:17, 25; 6:4; 20:24; 21:19; Rom. 11:13; 2 Cor. 3:7, 8, 9; 4:1; 5:18; 6:3; 9:1, 12; Eph. 4:12; Col. 4:17; 2 Tim. 4:5, 11) or "serve/service/serving" (Rom. 12:7; 15:31; 1 Cor. 12:5; 16:15; 2 Cor. 8:4; 9:13; 11:8; 1 Tim. 1:12; Rev. 2:19).
[4] The verb *diakoneo* is used thirty-seven times: "serves/served/serving/service" (Matt. 8:15; 20:28; Mark 1:31; 10:45; Luke 4:39; 10:40; 12:37; 17:8; 22:26, 27; John 12:2,

The greatest among you shall be your deacon. Whoever exalts himself will be humbled, and whoever humbles himself will be exalted. (Matt. 23:11–12)

And [Jesus] said to them, "If anyone would be first, he must be last of all and deacon of all." (Mark 9:35)

If anyone deacons me, he must follow me; and where I am, there will my deacon be also. If anyone deacons me, the Father will honor him. (John 12:26)

Above all, Christian believers are those who walk in the footsteps of the ultimate deacon, the suffering servant who came "not to be deaconed but to deacon, and to give his life as a ransom for many" (Mark 10:45).

In sum, *diakonos* is usually just a generic term for "servant"—hence the attribution to non-Christian rulers[5] and even to demons.[6] A small handful of times, though, the word is employed in a narrower, more technical sense—hence this book.[7]

To "deacon" in this narrower sense—which is how we typically understand the word and how I will use it from now on—is not an informal role. It isn't simply a ministry job title, like "campus director" or "children's ministry coordinator." It is one of two offices the New Testament establishes for the local

26; 2 Tim. 1:18; Philem. 13; Heb. 6:10; 1 Pet. 1:12; 4:10, 11) or "ministered/ministering" (Matt. 4:11; 27:55; Mark 1:13; 15:41) or "bringing aid" (Rom. 15:25).

[5] Rom. 13:4.

[6] 2 Cor. 11:15. (Kudos to Wake Forest University, home of the Demon Deacons, for being theologically astute!)

[7] Phil. 1:1; 1 Tim. 3:8, 12; possibly Rom. 16:1. See the first appendix for a discussion of the Romans passage. It's worth noting that this binary—generic service or formal office—isn't always helpful, since there aren't only two uses of *diakonos*. The recent work of Clarence D. Agan III demonstrates at least four uses of the term, as we will see in chapter 4.

church. Only elders (or pastors) and deacons are ordained to formal, public service in the life of the congregation.

How crucial, then, is diaconal service to church health? Crucial enough for God to carve out an official position for select members, recognized as model servants, to mobilize practical service in creative ways.

CONTRASTING CLONES

Clint and Tom are two pastors who couldn't have more in common. Same age, same theological degree, same denomination, same church size, same temperament, same basic level of spiritual maturity, same amount of ministry experience. And both of their churches are doing well. Growth isn't explosive, but it's steady. Conversions are happening. Their members are mostly happy. But while Clint is tired, Tom is tanked. For Clint, joy is a battle; for Tom, joy is a distant memory. Clint doesn't meet his sermon-deadline goal every week; Tom hasn't in a year. So what's the difference? What's draining Tom's time and energy? Hard thing is, it's always something different. But always something important.

- **Three weeks ago**, Tom had to purchase a new sound system for the church. He planned to spend an hour or two researching quality and cost-effective options, and then making a decision. It sucked up his entire Wednesday. *Zero energy left for anything else*, he thinks.
- **Two weeks ago**, Tom coordinated volunteers for a local park cleanup, an ideal yearly opportunity for the church to serve its neighbors and strike up gospel conversations. He created an online signup sheet, then notified the

church via email, then monitored the response, then got discouraged, then sent a few private requests, then realized Friday afternoon was over. *Sermon isn't nearly done, and thirteen empty slots remain for this stupid cleanup project. What's wrong with everyone?*

- **Last week**, Tom planned a welcome cookout for college students. This is one of his favorite times of the year. The university is a short walk from his church building, and as someone who got saved in college, Tom loves opportunities to reach incoming students. Or he used to. His excitement finally succumbs to disillusionment as he stands in the grocery-store aisle, adjudicating the merits of hot dog buns. *Wait, is the off-brand really more expensive? How is that even possible? I've got so much left to buy . . .*

- **This week**, Tom was a man resolved. *I will not get sidetracked. I will delegate. I can't be all things to all people.* His phone buzzes. Text from his wife. "Martha called. She's still in the hospital and wants you to come again. Said she hasn't heard from you this week." *It's only Tuesday morning!* "Also said she can't pay her bill. Apparently another patient is getting money from his church. Asked if we can help her."

Remember happy Clint? His month wasn't easy, but it was different. It was . . . manageable. So, again, what's the difference between the pastoral experiences of Clint and Tom? Answer: only one has deacons. Both do, actually, but only Clint's seem to know—and love—what being a deacon entails. They delight in relieving Clint from shouldering practical tasks so that he can channel his energies to the ministry of the Word and to prayer.

- Tom had to pore over countless customer reviews to find the right sound system. Clint has a deacon who was eager to do the needed research.
- Tom had to recruit volunteers for the park cleanup. Clint has a deacon who finds joy in gathering a team.
- Tom got stressed about hot dog buns. Clint has a deacon who is glad to run point on picking up groceries.
- Tom had to look at the church budget and assess giving trends in order to determine whether money can be spared for Martha. Clint has a deacon who excels at determining what the church can do to help financially.

The complexities of ministry are endless, aren't they? And when you add the fluidity of people's expectations to the immovable rock of limited time, you collide with some maddening math. I've witnessed this dynamic on both ends, in a sense, as I was privileged to serve in two diaconal positions before becoming an elder.

If you are an elder, and particularly if you are the primary preaching pastor in your church, internalize this: deacons wrongly deployed can *halve* your ministry, but deacons rightly deployed can *double* it. They can also build up the whole congregation—or not.

For better or for worse, deacons are difference-makers.

MANIFESTO AND MANUAL

In the coming chapters, we will consider many pressing questions about this sometimes misunderstood subject. I hope this book will serve as both a manifesto and a practical manual for ordinary churches like yours.

So here's where we are going. Chapter 1 will briefly sketch the various ways deacons have functioned throughout Christian history, as well as common (not necessarily healthy!) models in churches today. Chapter 2 will examine the forerunners to the office (Acts 6). Chapter 3 will then examine the qualifications for the office (1 Timothy 3). Following this discussion of what deacons must *be*, chapter 4 will zoom in on what deacons must *do*. In chapter 5, we will hear stories of real churches that have been strengthened by faithful diaconal service. Chapter 6 will consider the One whom deacons ultimately reflect, followed by a brief conclusion. The question of whether women may serve as deacons, or deaconesses, will be addressed in the first appendix. (Throughout the book I will use male pronouns for the sake of style and readability; but as you will see, I believe the diaconate is open to qualified women as well.) A second appendix will provide a sample questionnaire for prospective deacons.

The basic thesis of this book is that deacons—rightly understood and deployed—are an irreplaceable gift to Christ's church. They are model servants who excel in being attentive and responsive to tangible needs in the life of the church. In what ways do they serve? By assisting the elders, guarding the ministry of the Word, organizing service, caring for the needy, preserving unity, mobilizing ministry, and more.

A church without biblical deacons may exhibit signs of health for a while, but over time its health will suffer. We rob ourselves of the benefits of God's revealed wisdom when we either unduly *elevate* the role of deacons (say, to de facto elders) or unduly *reduce* their role (say, to glorified janitors).

Thankfully the Word of God charts a more excellent way. What it says about deacons is not extensive, but it is enough.

When deacons flourish, the whole congregation wins.

1

THE BACKSTORY
AND THE BLUNDERS:
HOW DEACONS HAVE
FUNCTIONED

The Nazis, it turns out, did not like deacons.

After the Netherlands fell to Germany in 1940, deacons in the Dutch Reformed Church rose up to care for the politically oppressed, supplying food and providing secret refuge. Realizing what was happening, the Germans decreed that the office of deacon should be eliminated. Responding in a General Synod on July 17, 1941, the Dutch believers resolved, "'Whoever touches the diaconate interferes with what Christ has ordained as the task of the church.' . . . Whoever lays hands on *diakonia* lays hands on worship!"[1]

The Germans backed down.

---

[1] In this opening section I am quoting (with only slight paraphrase) from Frederick Herzog's essay, "Diakonia in Modern Times, Eighteenth–Twentieth Centuries," in *Service in Christ*, ed. James I. McCord and T. H. L. Parker (Grand Rapids, MI: Eerdmans, 1966), 147. Thanks to Jonas Bültemann for tracking down the original German source and confirming the citation for me.

DEACONS THROUGH THE AGES

Most diaconal stories are, of course, less historically momentous. Rarely are they less beautiful. For two thousand years deacons have shone as they've served churches and communities around the globe. The witness of history is plain: a congregation without biblically functioning deacons is impoverished, but a congregation with them is incalculably rich.

How, then, have deacons functioned through the ages? The question is neither irrelevant nor dull; it is practical. If you are a follower of Jesus, then Christian history is *your* history. Studying it is like opening a photo album and flipping through your family heritage.

So let's begin. Embark with me on a flyover survey—admittedly fast and fragmentary—of the diaconal landscape since the apostolic age.

Early Church

Deacons were held in a place of honor in Christianity's earliest centuries. Based on the precedent of Acts 6:1–7—a passage generally seen to establish, or at least preview, the office—deacons in the early church were tasked with supporting the work of pastors by caring for the "outward" or "physical" concerns of church life.

Historian Rodney Stark notes that deacons in the early church were of "considerable importance," assisting in liturgical functions and administering the benevolent and charitable activities of the church.[2] A series of fourth-century treatises called the *Apostolic Constitutions* further outlined diaconal duties: "They are to be doers of good works, exercising a general supervision day and night, neither scorning the poor nor respecting the person of the rich; they must ascertain who are in distress and not exclude them from a share in church funds, compelling also the well-to-do to put money aside for good works."[3] Historian Charles Deweese aptly summarizes:

> They visited martyrs who were in prison, clothed and buried the dead, looked after the excommunicated with the hope of restoring them, provided the needs of widows and orphans, and visited the sick and those who were otherwise in distress. In a plague that struck Alexandria about AD 259, deacons were described by an eyewitness as those who "visited the sick fearlessly," "ministered to them continually," and "died with them most joyfully."[4]

Indeed, it was this kind of risky, self-giving love—modeled often by deacons—that bewildered the Roman world. As the African bishop Tertullian (AD 155–220) observed, "It is our care of the helpless, our practice of lovingkindness that brands us in the eyes of many of our opponents. 'Only look,' they say, 'look how they love one another!'"[5]

---

[2] Rodney Stark, *The Rise of Christianity: How the Obscure, Marginal Jesus Movement Became the Dominant Religious Force in the Western World in a Few Centuries* (San Francisco: HarperOne, 1997), 108. See also Robert Louis Wilken, *The First Thousand Years: A Global History of Christianity* (New Haven, CT: Yale University Press, 2012), 32.

[3] As quoted by Adolf Harnack, *The Mission and Expansion of Christianity in the First Three Centuries*, vol. 1 (New York: G. P. Putnam's Sons, 1908), 161. Also quoted in Stark, *Rise of Christianity*, 87.

[4] Charles Deweese, *The Emerging Role of Deacons* (Nashville: B&H, 1979), 12–13.

[5] Tertullian, *Apology* 39.

It is all too easy to lose sight of the spiritual value of deacons because their role is so practical in the life of the church. But many of the earliest deacons were giants of the faith, and they defended it with valor. Two stories must suffice.

First, let's travel to ancient Rome, epicenter of the mightiest empire on earth. Only eight years have passed since Emperor Decius sought to exterminate all who refused to pledge allegiance to his sovereign rule. Untold Christians were killed. It is now AD 258, and a man named Laurence is one of seven deacons serving in Rome; his task is to oversee the church's money and distributions to the poor. In August the news hits: Decius's successor, Valerian, has issued a chilling edict—all bishops, priests, and deacons must be rounded up and killed.

Laurence is soon taken before the magistrate. The offer: *surrender the treasure of the church, and you will be freed.* The deacon agrees. He only requests three days to retrieve it. Leaving the court, Laurence wastes no time. He entrusts the church's money to safe hands, and then gathers together the sick, the aged, the poor, the widowed, and the orphaned. At last he returns to the court, pitiful band in tow. Incensed by the commotion, the magistrate demands an explanation. Laurence responds, "Sir, I have brought what you asked for." Then, gesturing toward the people he's gathered, he declares, "These are the treasures of the church." Subsequently sentenced to a martyr's death, the deacon endures the flames with startling calm, even quipping to his executioners, "You may turn me over; I am done on this side." The spectacle of Laurence's profound courage makes a great impression on the people of Rome, leading to many conversions.[6]

Now fast-forward seventy years, and let's journey southeast to Telzeha (in modern-day Turkey). Persecution against Christians has again intensified, this time under Licinius. New emperor, new edict: *citizens must repair the altars and sacrifice to the god Jupiter*. What happens? A deacon rises up:

> Now Habib, who was of the village of Telzeha and had been made a deacon, went secretly into the churches in the villages. He ministered and read the Scriptures, encouraged and strengthened many by his words, and admonished them to stand fast in the truth of their belief and to not be afraid of the persecutors. . . .
>
> Many were strengthened by his words . . . and were careful not to renounce the covenant they had made. When the men appointed with reference to this particular matter heard of it, they informed [Licinius], the governor in the town of Edessa: "Habib, who is a deacon in the village of Telzeha, goes about and ministers secretly in every place, and resists the command of the emperors, and is not afraid."[7]

Not afraid indeed. Enduring a barrage of questions from the governor without wavering in his faith, Habib is burned

---

[6] This story may be apocryphal despite its wide circulation, with slightly varying details (except for the punchline!), ever since the fourth century. The earliest known source is Ambrose of Milan, *On the Duties of the Clergy*, book 2, ch. 28, sect. 140–41 (c. AD 391), in *A Select Library of the Nicene and Post-Nicene Fathers of the Christian Church*, Second Series, ed. Philip Schaff and Henry Wace, trans. W. H. Fremantle, G. Lewis, and W. G. Martley, vol. 10 (New York: Christian Literature Company, 1893). The annual calendar in the *Book of Common Prayer* (1662) designates August 10 as "Feast of St. Laurence, Deacon and Martyr at Rome, 258."

[7] "Martyrdom of Habib the Deacon," in *The Ante-Nicene Fathers*, ed. Alexander Roberts and James Donaldson, vol. 8 (New York: Charles Scribner's Sons, 1906), 690–95. I have updated the translation only slightly for readability. Interestingly, Emperor Licinius would later coauthor, along with his brother-in-law Constantine, the Edict of Milan in AD 313, granting official toleration to Christians throughout the Roman Empire.

at the stake. Stories like these offer a glimpse into the breath-taking conduct of the earliest deacons—and their steady yet staggering impact on the Roman world.

As the church sought to manage geographical expansion and as various heresies popped up to threaten the faith, a formalized hierarchy was developed to streamline—and centralize—decision-making authority within the office of bishop. So rather than only two church offices (bishops and deacons) there were now three: bishops (overseers), presbyters (elders or priests), and deacons. With the advent of this "monarchical episcopate" system—one bishop overseeing a geographic area—the primary role of deacons shifted from agents of charity to, essentially, secretaries to the bishop. They increasingly functioned as on-the-ground liaisons between the region's bishop and its local congregations.

Despite gradual distancing from the New Testament pattern, deacons continued to perform biblical tasks. Yet this didn't hold. Mark Dever summarizes the fateful decline:

> As the monarchical episcopate developed, so did a kind of monarchical diaconate beneath it. As the role of bishop developed, so did the role of archdeacon. The archdeacon was the chief deacon of a particular place and might be described as a deputy concerned with material matters. . . . Abuses eventually crept into the office of deacon, and deacons—especially archdeacons—became quite wealthy. How ironic that those who were meant to serve others instead used others to serve their own desires![8]

---

[8] Mark Dever, *Understanding Church Leadership*, Church Basics, ed. Jonathan Leeman (Nashville: B&H, 2016), 8–9.

Middle Ages

With this shift away from charitable work, two developments in the Middle Ages caused the diaconate to deteriorate even further.

First, the office was reduced to a mere steppingstone to the priesthood. Second, and more concerning, charitable giving came to be viewed as a means of saving one's soul and lessening another's time in purgatory. "By the Middle Ages," Cornelis Van Dam laments, "the chief motive for giving to the poor was to gain entrance to eternal life." The tragic downward spiral was complete, it seemed, as deacons soon "ceased to function in any biblical way."[9]

The time had come for a diaconal reformation.

John Calvin's Influence

No Reformer was more influential in restoring the diaconate to its ancient model—of ministering help to the poor and distressed—than John Calvin. Upon returning to Geneva in 1541, Calvin's first official act as pastor was to present to the city council a detailed plan for the order and governance of the church. These *Ecclesiastical Ordinances* called for the installation of deacons along with pastors, doctors (teachers), and elders. Historian Timothy George notes the "high esteem" in which Calvin held the diaconate:

> Deacons were public officers in the church entrusted with the care of the poor. He urged that they be skilled in the Christian

[9] Cornelis Van Dam, *The Deacon: Biblical Foundations for Today's Ministry of Mercy* (Grand Rapids, MI: Reformation Heritage, 2016), 99.

faith since, in the course of their ministry, "they will often have to give advice and comfort." . . . Calvin admitted that the diaconate could sometimes serve as a "nursery from which presbyters are chosen," yet he opposed the Roman custom of making the deacon the first step to the priesthood. This practice was an invidious undermining of "a highly honorable office."[10]

Under the leadership of Calvin, as well as contemporaries like Martin Bucer (1491–1551), deacons again began to serve not merely as protégés of priests but as ministers of mercy.

Reformation to Modern Era

Ever since Calvin gave fresh attention to the diaconate more than five centuries ago, the office has taken various shapes among Protestants.

- In the *Presbyterian and Reformed tradition*, deacons have always functioned mainly as mercy ministers, caring for the needy and distressed and often helping oversee the finances of the church.[11]
- In the *Anglican communion*, deacons are either "transitional," moving toward the priesthood,[12] or "vocational," appointed for life; all are theologically trained and formally ordained. In fact, every Anglican priest or bishop begins as a deacon, and none ever formally forsakes the office. Thus some archbishops have asked to be buried in their deacon

[10] Timothy George, *Theology of the Reformers*, rev. ed. (Nashville: B&H, 2013), 249.
[11] Elsie Anne McKee offers helpful historical perspective in *Diakonia in the Classical Reformed Tradition and Today* (Grand Rapids, MI: Eerdmans, 1989). For a modern evangelical treatment, see Van Dam, *The Deacon*.
[12] Speaking of the Church of England, Francis Young writes, "All ordained ministers in the Church of England are ordained to the diaconate before they are admitted to the priesthood" (Francis Young, *Inferior Office? A History of Deacons in the Church of England* [Cambridge: James Clarke & Co., 2015], xxv).

robes—the conviction being that if you cut open an arch-bishop, you find a bishop; if you cut open a bishop, you find a priest; and if you cut open a priest, you find a deacon. For diaconal service is at the heart of all ministry.[13]

- In many *congregational and baptistic churches*, a model of plural elders and deacons—the elders devoted to spiritual oversight, the deacons to practical service—largely endured until the early twentieth century, when many congregations began favoring a "solo pastor and deacon board" model, often accompanied by an array of committees. ("Of the making of many committees there is no end," a modern Ecclesiastes might read!) Yet this structure is not uniform, and in more recent years there seems to be a drive, among many such churches, to replace the executive-board mentality with a more historic vision for deacons. In this approach, deacons coordinate various ministries in the church, as a means of supporting the elders.[14]

---

[13] I am grateful to my friend Dan Marotta, rector of Redeemer Anglican Church in Richmond, Virginia, for bringing this anecdote to my attention. It is noteworthy, moreover, that anti-slavery activist Thomas Clarkson (1760–1846) was a deacon in the Church of England when he joined the abolitionist cause and campaigned alongside William Wilberforce. He helped to pass the Slave Trade Act of 1807, which ended the British slave trade. It is difficult to imagine a deacon making a more positive cultural impact on the nineteenth-century world. See Young, *Inferior Office?*, xxiii–xxiv.

[14] In an essay titled "Elders and Deacons in History," Mark Dever details the former prominence and subsequent decline of plural eldership in Baptist life. In summary he writes: "It is indisputable that at the beginning of the twentieth century, Baptists either had or advocated elders in local churches—and often a plurality of elders. They had done so for centuries. . . . Yet throughout the twentieth century, both the practice of plural eldership and the use of the title 'elder' grew increasingly scarce in Baptist life. To mention elders in many Baptist churches today would raise suspicions of being crypto-Presbyterian. But in the past few decades, the office of elder has seen a significant revival among Southern Baptists" (Mark Dever, "Elders and Deacons in History," in *Baptist Foundations: Church Government for an Anti-Institutional Age*, ed. Mark Dever and Jonathan Leeman [Nashville: B&H Academic, 2015], 238).

Dever then offers an anecdotal observation: "Many Southern Baptist churches increasingly sense that the present structures are simply not working. Some churches led by a single pastor suffer under an authoritarian rule too much like the Gentile leadership Jesus forbade in Mark 10:42. Other times young pastors have gone into churches and

BIBLICAL MODELS?

As mentioned earlier, the Bible doesn't say a great deal about deacons. (How's that for an incentive to keep reading?) Acknowledging this, however, should forge a twofold resolve: one, to pay extra careful attention to everything Scripture *does* teach on the topic; and, two, to treat those who see or "do" deacons differently with a special dose of generosity.

But even though the Bible's treatment of deacons is sparse, it is sufficient. We have enough scriptural material to judge between various approaches. And I'm convinced there are several common mindsets that fall short of God's soaring vision for the diaconate. Why is it so important we get this right? Not only so that we might experience swells of unity and joy in the churches we love, but also so that the servant nature of Jesus himself might be on full display.

Therefore, let's turn our attention to six popular conceptions of a deacon that fall short of the Bible's high vision for the office.

1. Pastor-in-Training Peter

"Heard they're making you a deacon. How long, you think, before they make you an elder?"

Peter is used to such questions at church. He's not bothered; if anything, he's a bit flattered.

We've already seen how, in the fourth century and into the Middle Ages, the diaconate had calcified into a mere entry-level

---

found them ossified, effectively ruled by deacons, a nominating committee, a personnel committee, or some other group that has no biblical standard of maturity in understanding and teaching the Scriptures" (240).

clergy role, a pit stop on the path to priesthood. The priest-in-training model remains common in the Roman Catholic Church and, despite key differences, in much of the Anglican communion as well. But some low-church evangelicals have their own version of this approach: elders in training. To be sure, certain deacons should eventually become elders—but that's assuming they meet the qualifications for *elders* (1 Tim. 3:1–7; Titus 1:5–9). And as we'll see in chapter 3, while the qualification lists for the two offices are similar, they are not the same.

Deaconing is not training wheels for eldering. It is a different office with different aims requiring, in many cases, different gifts. To take just one example, a man could lack the ability to teach—and therefore be unfit for eldership (1 Tim. 3:2; Titus 1:9)—and yet nonetheless be a truly spectacular deacon.

So, can Deacon Peter pursue pastoral ministry? Of course, but that should not be *why* he's a deacon. Every shepherd must first be a servant, yes, but not every servant is meant to become a formal shepherd. Diaconal service is too significant—too glorious—to be a mere stepping-stone toward anything else.

2. Toolbox Terrance

"You're good at fixing things. They should make you a deacon."

Many days, Pastor Jim is glad to have Terrance in the church. Terrance is a successful general contractor who may own more tools than the rest of the small church combined. What did Jim do when the church water heater broke three winters ago? He called Terrance. When the HVAC system sputtered out on that blistering Saturday in June? He called Terrance.

There is seemingly nothing Terrance can't find a way to fix. When it comes to tending the church's building and grounds, his know-how is unmatched.

Wouldn't Terrance make an ideal deacon? Not so fast. I haven't yet told you whether he's a mature believer. A deacon is far more than someone who knows his way around Home Depot. Does he know his way around his Bible?

3. Spreadsheet Sam

"Our church budget is a mess; we're looking at another financial shortfall and don't have any clear income projections for the next fiscal year. Why don't we make Sam a deacon—doesn't he fix people's money problems for a living?"

Sam's weekday-morning routine is not complicated: he wakes up, brews some coffee, and checks the market before hopping into the shower and heading to work at his financial-planning firm. On Sundays, it's not uncommon for church members to gingerly approach him for some casual financial advice. When it comes to shrewd economic sense, Sam is unrivaled in the church.

Wouldn't Sam make an ideal deacon? Again, not so fast. I haven't yet told you whether he's a mature believer. Spreadsheet wizardry is a welcome skill, but it's not sufficient for holding an office in God's home (1 Tim. 3:15).

4. Corporate Cliff

"Seminaries may teach ancient languages, bless their heart, but they can't teach executive skills. What this church really needs are some decisive deacons with business sense."

Cliff has been a member at Pinehill Community Church for thirty years and has served as a deacon for almost twenty. Around the time he joined the church he started a company in his basement; now it operates out of a skyscraper downtown. It's no secret Cliff has done well for himself in the marketplace. He's got scores of employees and decades of business savvy.

Isn't Cliff an ideal deacon? Once more, not so fast. I haven't yet told you whether he's a mature believer. Executive-leadership experience can be a serious asset, but it's no indication of spiritual fitness.

5. Veto Vinnie

"What's the point of being deacons if we're just 'yes men'? Of course, I tell Pastor Dave how it is—who else will? Besides, I only want to keep him humble. Last thing we need is a puffed-up pastor."

Deacon Vinnie is nothing if not a contrarian. He's not trying to make Pastor Dave's life miserable, though he often succeeds. He has simply taken it upon himself to keep the pastor grounded. Frankly, Vinnie doesn't want much about the church to change, but he can smell the desire for innovation wafting from the pastor's office. Just last week, Dave was "dreaming" of starting some pastoral internship and—*voilà! just like that!*—ending two longtime church programs in order to fund it.

Vinnie likes to carefully bubble-wrap his complaints. "Some people are talking" is a favorite. (It's important Pastor Dave knows it's not just Vinnie's concern.)

Isn't Vinnie an ideal deacon? I think we can agree he's not.

6. Pseudo-Elder Steve

"Welcome to First Baptist Church, where the pastors say things and the deacons run things. (Seriously, though, if you want to get something important done around here, you've got to convince those deacons.)"

Steve sits on the board of a few organizations; none gratifies him more than serving as a deacon at First Baptist. He loves the congregation and cares deeply about its long-term health. Steve is fine with the pastor leading the way on spiritual things—a paper hanging in his office claims he mastered divinity, after all—but it's the deacons' job to oversee everything else, right?

This sort of approach is not rare. I think of how one pastor-friend described to me the mindset he inherited in his church: "Basically, elders and deacons have separate but equal spheres of authority: elders govern the 'spiritual'; deacons govern the 'physical.' What does this mean practically? Deacons can't dictate what elders do with spiritual matters, since that's their lane; and elders can't dictate what deacons do with pragmatic matters, since that's *their* lane."

When deacons start to function either as leading shepherds over the whole congregation, or as a board of directors overseeing various staff and committees, the Bible's job description for deacons has become blurred. Further, any structure that encourages deacons to function as a counterweight to the pastor or elders—a second house of legislature to "check and balance" pastoral decisions—has overstepped its biblical bounds.[15] Though this may not have been the intention, far too often it is the effect.

TWO CAVEATS

At this point I want to be careful to acknowledge a couple of things. First, the intent behind this pseudo-elder/executive-board setup is rarely adversarial—it's rarely some powerplay to

---

[15] This model remains especially common in the Southern Baptist Convention—America's largest Protestant denomination, representing more than forty-seven thousand churches—despite decades of internal critique. Writing to Southern Baptists in the mid-twentieth century, Robert Naylor warned, "There is a 'board' complex and a general feeling that deacons are 'directors' of the church. Nothing could be farther from the Baptist genius or the New Testament plan" (Robert E. Naylor, *The Baptist Deacon: From a Pastor with a Special Heart for Deacons* [Nashville: B&H, 1955], 3). Howard Foshee, in his influential 1975 book *Now That You're a Deacon*, writes: "As a new deacon, you must understand that you have not been elected to an 'official board' to exercise authority in the life of the church. The office of deacon is not an office of authority but of service" (Howard B. Foshee, *Now That You're a Deacon* [Nashville: B&H, 1975], 13). Likewise, Henry Webb's *Deacons: Servant Models in the Church*—probably the most influential Southern Baptist book on deacons in the past forty years—details what will occur in a mature church: "The deacons will reject the role of the board of directors who are ultimately in charge of running everything, including telling the pastor what to do" (Henry Webb, *Deacons: Servant Models in the Church*, rev. ed. [Nashville: 1980; repr., B&H, 2001], 61).

How, though, did this unhelpful model originate? Webb envisions the scene: "The board role did not begin as a power grab on the part of the deacons. Possibly one hundred and fifty to two hundred years ago a couple of church members came out of a church house, one saying to the other: 'Ah, that was tough. I'm not sure I enjoy those business meetings. We have to discuss things that sometimes we differ on and sometimes we argue about. I think it would be great if we just asked the deacons to decide those things and tell us what we ought to do.' Thus was founded the board of directors approach to deacon ministry. There are two problems with the board role for deacons. The first problem is that the people are giving away a responsibility that they have no right to give away. The second problem is the deacons accept that responsibility. I think that the deacons accept that responsibility with good intentions, thinking they are serving the congregation. However, deacons are not really serving their congregations when they accept a controlling board role" (111). Additionally, Mark Dance, former executive editor of LifeWay's *Deacon Magazine*, remarks, "Some deacons assume a more supervisory role than a support role. [This began to happen over a century ago] when some churches began adopting a secular board model. This has unfortunately led to an unbiblical role-reversal with the office of pastor. Instead of washing his feet, this model encourages deacons to hold the pastor's feet to the fire" (Mark Dance, personal correspondence, March 31, 2020).

neutralize the pastor. If anything, the model is simply meant to capitalize on different strengths. And the Bible *does* point to a clear division of labor between pastors and deacons, which we'll explore in coming chapters. Their offices are not the same.

Second, some of us who believe the pseudo-elder/executive-board model falls short of God's design need to face the music: this configuration is often downstream from emergency situations in which a church's deacons were left scrambling for solutions and stepped up to fill a leadership vacuum in the wake of another departed pastor. To be sure, some churches have a revolving door of pastors because the deacons are insufferable. Still, what often occurs is a new pastor arrives—armed to the hilt with new energy! new vision! new initiatives!—only to become another episode in a very old series. Conflict arises. Eventually the pastor leaves. People assume he left for greener pastures. And who stays? Who always stays? The deacons. It's natural that a certain authority would accrue to the church's living furniture.

Many deacons who are stuck in unhelpful models are godly saints, doing their best to serve churches they've faithfully loved. Yes, I hope to convince them (you?) that there's a better way. Stay tuned. I simply wish to sound this note from the outset, because I mean it: deacon, if you haven't grasped for power but have risen to take responsibility in situations of unstable leadership, I am grateful for you.

CAVALRY OF SERVANTS

Whether the role of deacons in your church has been wrongly inflated or wrongly reduced, the solution is not to swing from one extreme to another, but to restore deacons to their intended biblical purpose and irreplaceable biblical role. Deacons are not the church's spiritual council of directors, nor the executive board to whom the pastor-CEO answers. They are the cavalry of servants, deputized to execute the elders' vision by coordinating various ministries. Deacons are like a congregation's Special Ops force, carrying out unseen assignments with fortitude and joy.

If you want to find a qualified deacon, don't look at his garage to see how many tools he has. Don't look at his financial portfolio to see how many investments he has. Don't look at his company to see how many employees he has. Look first at his attitude, his character, his life. Is he eager to listen, or is he angling to be heard? Is he humble and flexible, or does he always insist on his own way? Does he covet status, or does he yearn to serve? Gratefully, we don't have to improvise diaconal qualifications—the Bible provides them plainly; we'll examine them in chapter 3.

The Nazis were threatened by those Dutch deacons because of their gladhearted service and lionhearted faith. Those Roman emperors weren't big fans of deacons, either. And no wonder: Satan hates deacons and has sought to sideline them for two thousand years. Inconveniently for him, though, an omnipotent God loves them. The office of deacon was his invention, designed for the harmony and happiness of his people and the advancement of his kingdom.

And we see its first flickers in the New Testament's first church.

2

THE BLUEPRINT: WHERE DEACONS BEGAN

How are things going in your church? Is it everything you dreamed it would be?

If you're a pastor and you're nodding, I'm guessing it's your second month. Your shirt still bears the faint aroma of a seminary coffee shop. If you're smiling, you're probably in your second year. You reflect on your naïve idealism with a slight eyeroll. If you're crying, you're probably in your second decade. You still have a big ministry dream: it's called a sabbatical.

Of course I'm being facetious, but you get the point. Church ministry is often grueling, not glamorous. The stuff we daydreamed about is routinely not the stuff we spend our days doing. How many encouraging emails about your leadership or teaching have you received this week? If several, praise God! If none, welcome to the club.

In recent years there's been a flurry of books about returning to the simplicity of the early church, back to a time when Christians stayed on mission and loved each other. Isn't that what the book of Acts is about? The lost getting converted, the sick getting healed, and—miracle of miracles—the saints getting along? *Ah, if only we could rid ourselves of all this complexity and division and return to the glory days of Acts, when ministry was simple and the church was unified.*

This certainly seems to be the situation early on. Luke reports,

> [The church] devoted themselves to the apostles' teaching and the fellowship, to the breaking of bread and the prayers. And awe came upon every soul, and many wonders and signs were being done through the apostles. And all who believed were together and had all things in common. And they were selling their possessions and belongings and distributing the proceeds to all, as any had need. And day by day, attending the temple together and breaking bread in their homes, they received their food with glad and generous hearts, praising God and having favor with all the people. And the Lord added to their number day by day those who were being saved. (Acts 2:42–47)

What about two chapters later? How are things at this point? Still going swimmingly:

> The full number of those who believed were of one heart and soul, and no one said that any of the things that belonged to him was his own, but they had everything in common. And with great power the apostles were giving their testimony to the resurrection of the Lord Jesus, and great grace was upon them all. There was not a needy person among them. . . . (Acts 4:32–34)

And two chapters after that? Well, it's not so simple anymore. The church is still growing, but now some members are upset. Sound familiar?

CONFLICT BREWING

In Acts 6:1–7, Luke gives an updated report on the Jerusalem congregation:

> Now in these days when the disciples were increasing in number, a complaint by the Hellenists arose against the Hebrews because their widows were being neglected in the daily distribution. And the twelve summoned the full number of the disciples and said, "It is not right that we should give up preaching the word of God to serve tables. Therefore, brothers, pick out from among you seven men of good repute, full of the Spirit and of wisdom, whom we will appoint to this duty. But we will devote ourselves to prayer and to the ministry of the word." And what they said pleased the whole gathering, and they chose Stephen, a man full of faith and of the Holy Spirit, and Philip, and Prochorus, and Nicanor, and Timon, and Parmenas, and Nicolaus, a proselyte of Antioch. These they set before the apostles, and they prayed and laid their hands on them.
>
> And the word of God continued to increase, and the number of the disciples multiplied greatly in Jerusalem, and a great many of the priests became obedient to the faith.

Phew, we sigh. *That was a close call.*

It might be easy to think the threat here wasn't really *that* serious, especially since Luke is so careful to bookend the story with glad news of conversion growth (vv. 1a, 7). But that's not how the bookends are meant to function:

- "the disciples were increasing in number" (v. 1a)
  - "a complaint arose . . ." (vv. 1b–6)
- "And the word of God continued to increase, and the number of the disciples multiplied greatly" (v. 7)

As we read the story, verse 7 is not a foregone conclusion. It isn't the natural, expected outcome. Had the conflict been mishandled, the ending could easily have read, "And the word of God was compromised, as the disciples divided among themselves." Luke's wording, then, is a ringing declaration that disaster has been averted and fruitful ministry can proceed unhindered.

Our ministry daydreams tend to mirror verse 7 ("the number of the disciples multiplied"), don't they? Many of our ministry days, however, are occupied by verse 1b ("a complaint arose"). So Luke structures the story to make it plain: the joy of verse 7 rarely comes without the work of verses 2–6. Indeed, how our churches react to conflict can make all the difference in whether our gospel witness is obstructed or accelerated. Acts 6 is a story of church conflict handled well.

And it has everything to do with deacons.

THE SEVEN

You will look in vain for the noun "deacons" in Acts 6. Yet as we'll consider in a moment, the verbal form of the word shows up several times. Plus, biblical scholars have long understood the seven to provide a pattern for the diaconal office.[1] These men are forerunners who essentially preview the formal role

---

[1] "When all factors have been considered, it seems best to understand the ordination in Acts 6 as to an office that would later be called deacon. Although they are not called deacons here, the first readers of Acts may have seen the seven as deacons. This identification of the seven as the first ordained deacons has been the mainline position of the Christian church since the second century" (Cornelis Van Dam, *The Deacon: Biblical Foundations for Today's Ministry of Mercy* [Grand Rapids, MI: Reformation Heritage, 2016], 51).

that deacons will soon hold in local churches (e.g., Phil. 1:1; 1 Tim. 3:8–12).

So what can we learn about deacons from a story that never mentions the office? Plenty, in fact.

As we've seen, tension erupts—or finally surfaces—in the congregation when some Grecian Jews, called Hellenists, file "a complaint" against their Hebraic counterparts (v. 1). Apparently, their own widows were "being neglected in the daily food distribution" (v. 1b).

Surely we could imagine the apostles rebuking these angsty Hellenists. In just the previous chapter, after all, Peter publicly denounced Ananias and Sapphira for their deception (5:1–11), and the apostles stared down the high priest himself: "We must obey God rather than men. The God of our fathers raised Jesus, whom you killed by hanging him on a tree" (5:29–30). These were not wimpy, mealy-mouthed individuals. So we can imagine the rebuke: *Don't you see how well things are going? Can you not be content? And besides, this church is about Jesus; why are you focusing on yourselves?*

But no one says that, or anything like it. We should therefore not assume this was simply a ridiculous protest over a minor issue. It certainly wasn't treated that way.[2] The moment the apostles catch wind of "division endangering the joy of

---

[2] Van Dam explains, "The neglect of widows was a serious matter. Once a widow became a Christian and was likely expelled from the synagogue (see John 9:22; 12:42), she gave up the material security the synagogue had provided and could no longer benefit from its aid to the indigent. A Christian widow, then, needed help immediately. To be left unattended was unconscionable. . . . If there was one place where widows should feel completely at home in the present world, it was in the church" (Van Dam, *The Deacon*, 49, 50).

redemption,"[3] they spring into action, summoning "the full number of the disciples"—which by this time could have approximated eight thousand! So we're now looking at the Bible's first megachurch *and* something akin to its first members' meeting. Addressing this sea of saints, the apostles declare,

> It is not right that we should give up preaching the word of God to serve tables. Therefore, brothers, pick out from among you seven men of good repute, full of the Spirit and of wisdom, whom we will appoint to this duty. But we will devote ourselves to prayer and to the ministry of the word. (6:2b–4)

At least four things are worth observing here:

1. "Word Ministry" Prioritized

John Stott insightfully proposes that Acts 6 showcases a last-gasp satanic ploy, the culmination of a three-front assault. Satan's first two attempts—persecution from the outside (4:1–22) and moral corruption from within (5:1–11)—had utterly failed to destroy the church:

> The devil's next attack was the cleverest of the three. Having failed to overcome the church by either persecution or corruption, he now tried *distraction*. If he could preoccupy the apostles with social administration, which though essential was not their calling, they would neglect their God-given responsibilities to pray and to preach, and so leave the church without any defense against false doctrine.[4]

---

[3] Van Dam, *The Deacon*, 49.

[4] John Stott, *The Message of Acts: The Spirit, the Church, and the World* (1990; repr., Downers Grove, IL: IVP Academic, 1994), 120, emphasis added.

Without downplaying the importance of caring for widows, the apostles clarify the focus of their own labors. They will devote their best energy to shepherding the church by means of teaching and prayer. Note the play on words, rendered literally:

> It is not right that we should give up preaching the word of God to *deacon* tables. . . . But we will devote ourselves to prayer and to *deaconing* the word. (Acts 6:2, 4)

Read hastily, this might seem rather callous. Do the apostles lack concern for the welfare of the vulnerable? Are they elevating "spiritual" ministry above "practical" ministry—or perhaps not recognizing the latter as real ministry at all?

Absolutely not. By prioritizing Scripture and prayer, the apostles are choosing to stay focused on the whole church's spiritual welfare, even as they affirm the Hellenists' physical needs.[5] (They more than affirm the needs, in fact; they take the initiative to set in motion a permanent, structural solution.) Nevertheless, the apostles recognize a fundamental truth: a church whose ministers are chained to the tyranny of the urgent—which so often shows up in "tangible problems"—is a church removing its heart to strengthen its arm. It's a kind of slow-motion suicide.

A church without deacons may lack health, but a church without biblical preaching cannot exist. There is, in fact, no such thing.

---

[5] "There is no hint whatever that the apostles regarded social work as inferior to pastoral work, or beneath their dignity. It was entirely a question of calling. They had no liberty to be distracted from their own priority task" (Stott, *Message of Acts*, 121).

As the New Testament unfolds and more churches are established, the role of elders will come to be described similarly to that of the apostles. This is not to suggest that elders are equivalent to apostles; important differences exist.[6] Still, there is an evident correlation between both (1) apostles and elders[7] and (2) "the seven" and deacons.

2. Whole Congregation Involved

Notice that the twelve don't unilaterally select the seven; instead, they involve the whole church. (The "brothers" addressed in verse 3 are the "full number of the disciples" summoned in verse 2.)

Why would a decision of such import include ordinary saints, many of whom were brand-new converts? Two reasons come to mind, one theological and one practical. First, these church members are saved. Through trust in Christ, the Holy Spirit has taken up residence in their hearts. They are qualified, therefore, to pass judgment on matters in Christ's church because they have his Spirit. Second, and practically, these believers are directly invested in the outcome of the decision. This is their church, after all, and these are their fellow members. The seven men chosen won't simply have

---

[6] Unlike the office of elder, I believe, the office of apostle ceased at the death of the apostles. Sometimes the New Testament uses the word "apostle" informally to describe the "sent" status of all believers (e.g., Phil. 2:25); usually, however, it functions as a technical term for a formal—and, I believe, temporary—office. Apostles were identified by at least two criteria: (1) they were eyewitnesses of Jesus, or close associates of an eyewitness; and (2) they were personally commissioned by Jesus. Consider, for example, the operative logic in passages like Acts 1:21–26; 1 Cor. 9:1; 15:7; and 2 Pet. 1:16.

[7] For more on the role of elders, see Jeramie Rinne's superb book in this series, *Church Elders: How to Shepherd God's People Like Jesus* (Wheaton, IL: Crossway, 2014).

an effect on neglected widows; they will influence the entire body.

How beautiful, Cornelis Van Dam notes, that "the entire congregation had to participate in finding a solution, even though the problem was with only a part of the congregation."[8] Many members, one body.

To be clear, congregational involvement is not at odds with a church's pastors taking a leading role. For example, here's how the process of appointing deacons typically plays out in my own church:

1. Elders keep an eye out for deacon-qualified candidates in light of specific diaconal needs.
2. Elders always welcome, and periodically solicit, deacon recommendations from the congregation.
3. Elders select a candidate and send a questionnaire (see appendix 2).
4. Assuming the candidate's willingness and the elders' continued confidence in the choice, they nominate the candidate to the congregation at a members' meeting.
5. The congregation is given a month to privately ask questions and get to know the candidate, if desired.
6. At the next month's members' meeting, the congregation votes on whether to appoint the candidate to the office.

This last step, by the way, is no mere formality. The congregation has real access to the emergency brake, even as the elders steer the wheel. Nonetheless, an emergency brake is rarely utilized in a healthy vehicle. Indeed, it is a serious spiritual

---

[8] Van Dam, *The Deacon*, 53.

deficiency when a church has either "leaders who are untrustworthy or members who are incapable of trusting."[9]

3. Character Mandated

According to verse 3, diaconal candidates must be

- **"of good repute."** In other words, they are to be respectable, known for both character and conduct. The apostle Paul will "double-click" on this virtue in 1 Timothy 3:8–12, where he demands that deacons be "dignified," or "worthy of respect" (NIV). Look for an extended discussion of this passage in our next chapter.
- **"full of the Spirit."** As Christians, they will be indwelt by the Holy Spirit; as mature Christians, they must be known for submitting to the Spirit's leadership in their lives. These are not believers who fancy themselves as having spiritually arrived; on the contrary, they've reckoned with their weaknesses and are daily resolving to lean on the omnipotent Spirit of God.
- **"full of wisdom."** To be filled with the Spirit is to be filled, increasingly, with wisdom. He is, after all, the "Spirit of wisdom" (Eph. 1:17), who generously promises this gift to believers who ask (James 1:17; cf. 1 Cor. 2:13; Col. 1:9). Such wisdom is not some airy-fairy virtue, either. The church's chief servants should be known for exercising practical wisdom.

Needless to say, the seven were not spiritual slouches; they were gold-standard servants. In the words of Alexander

---

[9] Mark Dever, *Understanding Church Leadership*, Church Basics, ed. Jonathan Leeman (Nashville: B&H, 2016), 37.

Strauch, "The congregation chose its best to care for its least."[10]

4. Labor Divided

As we've seen, the apostles don't minimize the Hellenists' complaint. Rectifying the issue, in fact, is viewed not as an option but as a "duty" (Acts 6:3). Nevertheless, they believe the interests of the whole church—widows included—will be best served through a strategic division of labor. Rather than risk getting distracted from the ministry of the Word and prayer, the apostles deputize a separate group to coordinate a resolution to the problem.

This was not a separation into two spiritual teams, one varsity and one junior varsity. Thabiti Anyabwile's observation here is stirring:

> To modern sensibilities, "serving tables" sometimes connotes a low-level, demeaning position. A person waits tables when he or she is working through college, or passing time until a career takes off. People regard it as a necessary sacrifice to make ends meet.
>
> But how different it is in the Lord's church! The apostles under the inspiration of God's Spirit appear to have created an entirely new office in the church for the specific purpose of serving tables. And the loftiness of the office is seen in (a) the character of the individuals required to fill it ("full of the Spirit and of wisdom," v. 3), (b) the fact that this facilitates the ministry of Word and prayer, and (c) the unifying

---

[10] Alexander Strauch, *Paul's Vision for the Deacons* (Colorado Springs: Lewis & Roth, 2017), 82n1.

and strengthening effect it has on the whole church. The deaconate is important![11]

The strategic division of labor modeled in Acts 6 was a sign of strength in the first church, and it signals strength in churches today. Pastors (or deacons, for that matter) who try to do everything end up doing a disservice to everyone.

DEACONS ARE SHOCK ABSORBERS

Of the many lessons for deacons from Acts 6, perhaps most overlooked is their strategic role in preserving congregational unity. The seven weren't merely deployed to solve a food problem. Food was the occasion, sure, but it wasn't the deepest problem. The deepest problem was a sudden threat to church unity.

Acts 6 is a remarkable model for navigating local-church conflict, especially given the parties involved: Hellenists and Hebrews. Hellenists (v. 1) were Jews who had immigrated to Jerusalem from other parts of the Roman Empire. Many had likely come for Pentecost and planned to return home after the festival, not expecting to hear a message that would forever change the trajectory of their lives. Luke tells us that at Peter's preaching three thousand persons were converted, baptized, and added to the Jerusalem church (Acts 2:41)—surely this would have included many Hellenists who had since chosen to stay in Jerusalem. (It isn't as if there were other churches back home—this was the first one.)

---

[11] Thabiti Anyabwile, *Finding Faithful Elders and Deacons* (Wheaton, IL: Crossway, 2012), 20–21.

The Hebrews, meanwhile, were not "outsiders"; they had grown up on Palestinian soil. Thus they saw themselves as more authentically Jewish than these Hellenist newcomers who were more fluent in the language of pagans than the language of Jesus.[12] And yet the differences were not limited to language; they also encompassed ethnicity and culture.[13] Even secular historians at the time wrote about the animosity that existed between these groups, despite their common Jewish religion.[14]

This is why Acts 6 is far more than a culinary quibble. The apostles were faced with a natural fault line that threatened to fracture the very unity Christ died to achieve. The gospel insists, after all, that our unity in Christ supersedes any worldly difference. So make no mistake: the apostles did not delegate this problem to others because it *wasn't* important, but because it *was*. They could have imposed a swift, superficial solution and moved on. Instead they laid groundwork for an ongoing solution and a permanent church office.

How, then, did the congregation respond? Don't rush past verse 5:

> And what [the apostles] said pleased the whole gathering, and they chose Stephen, a man full of faith and of the Holy Spirit,

---

[12] That is, fluent in Greek instead of Aramaic. See I. Howard Marshall, *The Acts of the Apostles: An Introduction and Commentary* (Grand Rapids, MI: Eerdmans, 1988), 125–26.
[13] Stott writes, "The [Grecian Jews] not only spoke Greek but thought and behaved like Greeks, while the [Hebraic Jews] not only spoke Aramaic but were deeply immersed in Hebrew culture. . . . There had always, of course, been rivalry between these groups in Jewish culture; the tragedy is that it was perpetuated within the new community of Jesus who by his death had abolished such distinctions" (Stott, *Message of Acts*, 120–21).
[14] K. C. Hanson and Douglas E. Oakman, *Palestine in the Time of Jesus: Social Structures and Social Conflicts* (Minneapolis: Augsburg Fortress, 1998), 149.

and Philip, and Prochorus, and Nicanor, and Timon, and Par-
menas, and Nicolaus, a proselyte of Antioch.

What's the significance of this list? Why did Luke bother to
record these names? Likely because *they are all Greek names!*

This is remarkable. You can almost envision the head-
line: "Majority-Hebrew Congregation Chooses Seven Hellenist
Leaders." The very minorities feeling the sting of unfair food
distribution are the ones given a voice, tasked and empowered
to make decisions on behalf of the whole church.[15]

This list of names is the hidden punchline of the whole
story. The Hebrews in the church apparently prized unity so
much that they bent over backwards to care for their Hellenist
sisters—even to the point of entrusting their *own* widows to
these brothers from an unfamiliar Greek culture.

The selection of the seven was not about political cor-
rectness or meeting an arbitrary quota; it was about covenant
solidarity and "outdoing others" in showing honor (Rom.
12:10).

Given the root problem facing the seven, we can conclude
that deacons should be those who *muffle* shockwaves, not
make them reverberate further. Quarrelsome persons make
poor deacons, for they only compound the kind of headaches
deacons are meant to relieve. The best deacons, therefore,
are far more than business managers or handymen. They are
persons with fine-tuned "conflict radars." They love solutions

---

[15] Marshall writes, "It seems probable that the men appointed were drawn from the Greek-speaking part of the church which had raised the original complaint.... The seven names are all Greek, which suggests that their bearers were not Palestinian Jews" (Marshall, *The Acts of the Apostles*, 125, 127).

more than drama and rise to respond, in creatively construc-
tive ways, to promote the harmony of the whole.

Tracing the implications of Acts 6, Mark Dever and Paul
Alexander offer an apt summary:

> Deacons, then, serve to care for the physical and financial needs
> of the church, and they do so in a way that heals divisions,
> brings unity under the Word, and supports the leadership of the
> elders. Without this practical service of the deacons, the elders
> will not be freed to devote themselves to praying and serving
> the Word to people. Elders need deacons to serve practically,
> and deacons need elders to lead spiritually.[16]

DEACONS ARE PROBLEM SOLVERS

One final lesson for deacons emerges from this story. We've
already noted the apostles' delegation and the congregation's
involvement, even authority, in the decision-making process.
But not only do the apostles not tell the church whom to select,
they also don't tell those selected what to do. The seven are
deployed to solve the food-distribution problem, but they are
given no detailed instructions *how*. No wonder they need to be
"full of wisdom" (v. 3)!

Deacons shouldn't merely have a desire to safeguard unity.
They should also have a knack for solving problems; specifically, solving problems *in order to* safeguard unity. On top of
the character requirements for the office (1 Tim. 3:8–12),
then, an ideal deacon candidate should have a track record of
embodying and encouraging this cycle:

---

[16] Mark Dever and Paul Alexander, *The Deliberate Church: Building Your Ministry on the
Gospel* (Wheaton, IL: Crossway, 2005), 132.

sees a problem
→ wants to safeguard unity
→ thinks creatively
→ solves the problem

The seven were given considerable freedom in how to address the problem facing the Jerusalem church. The same should be true of deacons today. The arrangement works, though, only if these servants are known for solving problems rather than perpetuating them.

QUIET WORK, PROFOUND EFFECT

A deacon's work is often quiet, but its effect is profound. Luke doesn't want us to miss this. As we saw earlier, what followed the crisis and the constitution of the diaconate?

> And the word of God continued to increase, and the number of the disciples multiplied greatly in Jerusalem, and a great many of the priests became obedient to the faith. (v. 7)

Acts 6:1–7 isn't simply a paradigm for diaconal service. It's also a reminder that the work of deacons, though often focused on physical and administrative needs, has enormous spiritual implications. There is an inseparable link between the labor of a deacon and the flourishing of the Word. Public ministry is impossible without private service. Had the seven not freed the apostles to focus on teaching and prayer (v. 4), the gospel would not have spread (v. 7).

The work of a deacon, then, is freighted with significance. Its effects will reverberate into eternity. Beware of limiting your view of deacons to manual labor and Excel spreadsheets. Stephen was one of the seven, and in the next chapter he becomes the church's first martyr. Philip was one of the seven, and in two chapters he's declaring the gospel to Samaritans (8:4–8) and African court officials (8:26–40). He even makes an eventual appearance in Paul's travelogue: "On the next day we departed and came to Caesarea, and we entered the house of Philip the evangelist, who was one of the seven, and stayed with him" (Acts 21:8). Being part of the seven didn't confine Philip to serving tables. Though not an apostle, the brother was such a gospel-sharing machine that he became known not simply as "Philip the deacon" but as "Philip the evangelist."

The Bible's view of deacons is glorious. Let's not settle for less.

3

THE BASELINES:
WHAT DEACONS MUST BE

Imagine an ordinary church. We'll call it Middletown Community. Several folks in the congregation are known and respected, though for different reasons. Leroy is the most successful businessman. Shelby is the biggest giver. Keith can fix anything. Alex has been around for forty years. Juan hopes to eventually become an elder.

Is any of them qualified to be a deacon?

One of the tragedies in church life today is the lack of attention given to what biblical deacons are—and are not. Many churches seem content to continue operating from custom and tradition on this subject, with Bibles closed.

To be fair, I understand the hesitations:

- "I don't have the energy to rock the boat. That didn't go so well last time."
- "A wise leader has to pick his battles. Surely this isn't *that* pressing."
- "If it ain't broke, why fix it?"

Such reasoning *can* represent the way of wisdom. The ecclesial landscape is littered with the wreckage of churches whose
leaders either moved too fast on a major issue or gave a minor
issue a promotion it didn't deserve. So I'm not questioning the
motives or instincts of gospel-loving pastors who are hesitant
to shepherd their flock toward a different understanding of
deacons. It's certainly easier said than done.

And yet, we must all face the uncomfortable fact that Jesus
doesn't mince words when addressing leaders who cling to
tradition on matters where God has spoken (e.g., Matt. 15:1–
9). And a deacon's character is something on which God has
spoken.

Ignoring what the Bible says about deacons is not only
shortsighted or wrong, though. It's also strange. Why?
Because the Bible doesn't say much about deacons. Again,
shouldn't this be all the more reason to take seriously the
revelation we do have?

NOT PRIVATE AND NOT OPTIONAL

The letter we call 1 Timothy is not a private note to a pen
pal. Paul writes to Timothy personally, yes, but not privately.
The apostle designs his letter as a public document to guide
all churches, not just Timothy's flock in Ephesus. Culturally
rooted does not mean culturally relative.

The first hint of universal applicability is seen in the
way Paul prefaces his instructions for gathered worship: "I
desire that in every place . . ." (1 Tim. 2:8). In other words,
"What I'm writing to you, Timothy, is applicable *everywhere*,

not just in Ephesus."[1] But Paul's clearest statement comes in the next chapter:

> I hope to come to you soon, but I am writing these things to you so that, if I delay, you may know how one ought to behave in the household of God, which is the church of the living God, a pillar and buttress of the truth. (1 Tim. 3:14–15)

If 1 Timothy has a purpose statement, surely this is it. Notice three things.

1. Paul's instructions in this letter are *to* Timothy but they are *for* everybody. Notice his concern is with how "one"— that is, any person (NIV "people"), not just Timothy— should lead God's church.
2. Paul is not offering suggestions, strategic ideas, or "best practices." Timothy is holding a letter of divinely inspired commands. Notice Paul doesn't say that he's merely revealing how a person *could* or *might* behave in church. He says *ought*, a word brimming with moral force.
3. What are "these things" that are meant to govern church practice? I believe Paul is referring to the contents of the whole letter, but what is the immediate context? What are the morally binding "things" he's just addressed? The qualifications for deacons.

After listing the marks of eligibility for the office of overseer[2] in verses 1 to 7, Paul turns his attention to the office of deacon in verses 8 to 13.

---

[1] Also don't miss how Paul ends the letter: "Grace be with you" (1 Tim. 6:21). The "you" is plural, indicating that he's not addressing Timothy alone.
[2] Or "elder" or "pastor." Despite slightly different emphases, the three words are interchangeable in the New Testament and refer to the same office in the local church (compare Acts 20:17, 28; Titus 1:5, 7; 1 Pet. 5:1–2).

Deacons likewise must be dignified, not double-tongued, not addicted to much wine, not greedy for dishonest gain. They must hold the mystery of the faith with a clear conscience. And let them also be tested first; then let them serve as deacons if they prove themselves blameless. Their wives [or "the women"[3]] likewise must be dignified, not slanderers, but sober-minded, faithful in all things. Let deacons each be the husband of one wife, managing their children and their own households well. For those who serve well as deacons gain a good standing for themselves and also great confidence in the faith that is in Christ Jesus.

So should Leroy, Shelby, Keith, Alex, or Juan be installed as a deacon at Middletown Community Church? Perhaps. But the answer rests not on their previously listed attributes but on whether their lives embody this all-important paragraph.

THE MEASURE OF A DEACON'S LIFE

Perhaps the most surprising thing here is Paul's relative disinterest in what potential deacons are able to *do*. This paragraph is not about a skill set. Its focus is squarely on who deacons must *be*. (Don't miss this easy-to-forget lesson: God cares more about character than about gifting.[4])

The diaconal requirements are divided into three "negatives" and three "positives"—but first, one flies like a banner

---

[3] See the first appendix ("May Women Serve as Deacons?") for a discussion of this verse.
[4] Gregg Allison and Ryan Welsh are right: "Often, unfortunately, the qualification requirements . . . are replaced by urgent pragmatism: enticed by time limitations and human gifting, pastors can harmfully install leaders who are gifted but not qualified" (Gregg Allison and Ryan Welsh, *Raising the Dust: "How-To" Equip Deacons to Serve the Church* [Louisville: Sojourn Network, 2019], 11).

over the whole list: deacons must be "dignified" (NIV "worthy of respect"). This doesn't mean they must be perfect; it signifies they must be humble, repentant, and exemplars for the flock. So what does it look like, practically, to be dignified? The passage points to six things.

Paul lists the "negative" requirements first—what a deacon must *not* be. All three relate to a particular fruit of the Spirit: self-control.

1. Not Double-Tongued

Qualified deacons strive to control their tongues. Because deacons are in the business of serving, they will have countless interactions with people. And these interactions won't always be with the shiniest saints. Deacons will often be confronted with sufferers and strugglers, some of whom will be disgruntled and prone to complaining.

In all these interactions, a deacon must be compassionate while remaining vigilantly on guard. Deacons who are fulfilling the biblical role will:

- Guard their *tongues* from disclosing information that the person being served either should not know or simply doesn't need to know. *"Yeah, Pastor Mike can be like that sometimes. Just between us, it's a big struggle even for some of us deacons."*
- Guard their *ears* from being party to gossip or slander against church leaders or fellow members. *"Oh really? She said that? I was suspicious already, but I'll definitely keep my distance now!"*
- Guard their *tongues* (again) from gossip or slander as they recount conversations or information to others. It's

> difficult, after hearing something sensitive or "juicy," not
> to pass it along—perhaps couching it as a "prayer request."
> *"Bless his heart, we really need to pray for Earl—he still can't
> seem to get it together."*

Being double-tongued is not a minor flaw or personality quirk; it is a symptom of hypocritical pride. It's consciously saying one thing to one group—and then saying or insinuating something else to a different group. A double tongue indicates fear of man, and a deacon driven by the fear of man can destroy a whole church.

Flattery, it has been observed, is saying to someone's face what you wouldn't say behind their back, whereas gossip is saying behind someone's back what you wouldn't say to their face.[5] A qualified deacon studiously avoids both. But to the extent that a deacon lives to please people, this will prove impossible, for only the fear of God can drive out the fear of man.

Satan will do anything he can to gain a foothold in his Enemy's home (Eph. 4:27). A mature deacon won't use words to crack the door.

2. Not Addicted to Much Wine

Not only are deacons to be self-controlled in their speech, they're also to be self-controlled in their appetites. This standard prohibits drunkenness (cf. Eph. 5:18) and also challenges anything that would enslave the deacon's heart or impair his judgment.

---

[5] R. Kent Hughes, *Disciplines of a Godly Man*, tenth anniversary ed. (Wheaton, IL: Crossway, 2006), 139.

It's possible that Paul included this qualification since the nature of diaconal work would at times include bringing wine to the sick for medicinal reasons (1 Tim. 5:23). But whatever the purpose, the principle is plain: qualified deacons will not indulge cravings or abuse substances that would hinder their work or their witness.

3. Not Greedy for Dishonest Gain

Deacons carrying out the biblical mandate will control their speech, their appetites, and also their wallets (specifically, what goes *into* their wallets). While these virtues mark any mature believer, the specific nature of diaconal work will sometimes put deacons in contact with church money. So Paul warns against installing anyone known for being deceptive, cutting moral corners, or obsessing over money. A worldly, materialistic person will struggle with greed, which will in turn fuel temptation toward dishonest gain. This should be an area, then, where a deacon displays unimpeachable self-control.

After listing these three "negative" requirements, Paul then turns his attention to three "positive" ones.

4. Holds the Mystery of the Faith with a Clear Conscience

It can be easy to assume that deacons—given the practical focus of their work—don't need to know much doctrine. *Deacon work is hand work, not head work*, one might think. *Can't they just stay in their lane and outsource theology to the pastors?* Not according to Scripture. It's true that the primary responsibility for teaching and governing falls to the church's elders—and the roles of elders and deacons must not be confused—but deacons are not exempt from knowing their Bibles. In fact, they will often be in situations where they will have opportunity to speak biblical truth. The question, then, is not whether deacons will be theologians; it's whether they will be good ones.

When Paul uses the word "mystery," as he often does, he's not referring to a genre of Roman novels. He's referring to divine truth that was once hidden and is now revealed. He's referring to the content of the gospel and Christian doctrine. Notice that this brief qualification actually demands three things of potential deacons:

- They must *know* the faith. This is implicit and obvious, for one cannot hold what one does not know. A qualified deacon will be eager to grow in a clear understanding of God, humanity, Christ, salvation, and so on. This doesn't mean a deacon must be the biggest reader in the church, but it does mean he'll be hungry to learn the things of God.
- They must *hold* the faith. Whatever truth a deacon grasps with his mind, he must cling to with his heart. Anyone embarrassed by biblical truths that collide with current cultural trends is not yet qualified to serve as a deacon. God's Word is precious; look for those who embrace it with humble gladness.
- They must *live* the faith. It is not enough to know and to hold what's true; Paul also insists that a deacon's conscience must be clear.[6] This refers back to previous qualifications, of course, since hypocrisy—whether expressed in duplicitous speech, secret addictions, or dishonest profits—will slowly

---

[6] For a helpful book on the conscience, see Andrew David Naselli and J. D. Crowley, *Conscience: What It Is, How to Train It, and Loving Those Who Differ* (Wheaton, IL: Crossway, 2016). For a much briefer treatment, see Kevin DeYoung, *The Art of Turning: From Sin to Christ for a Joyfully Clear Conscience* (LaGrange, KY: 10Publishing, 2017).

shatter a clear conscience. But a deacon with a clear conscience will be a person of moral integrity and courage. I'm reminded of Atticus Finch's words in Harper Lee's *To Kill a Mockingbird*: "The one thing that doesn't abide by majority rule is a person's conscience."[7] Clarity of conscience is not the ultimate standard, since consciences are fallen, but it is an important one. A deacon with a healthy conscience will keep short accounts with God through genuine, ongoing confession and repentance (cf. 1 John 1:9).

5. Tested and Proven

How many times has a church been harmed by a deacon who had no business being one? And how many of those times could the disaster have been prevented by heeding the qualification about being "tested" and "proven blameless"?

One reason this standard can get sidelined, I imagine, is because Paul isn't explicit about the length or nature of the testing. What should the process entail and how long should it last? Individual churches must exercise wisdom and prayerful discernment. What is nonnegotiable, however, is that there should be a season of testing.

In my own church, as mentioned earlier, at least three steps must occur before someone becomes a deacon. First, the elders will discuss whether the person would be a good fit for the position. If we agree he would be, we will then invite him, assuming he desires to serve, to complete a questionnaire (see appendix 2). This valuable document gives the elders a better sense of the candidate's convictions and practices, strengths

---

[7] Harper Lee, *To Kill a Mockingbird* (New York: Grand Central, 1960), 140.

and weaknesses. Finally, we will nominate the person in a members' meeting, encouraging the church to take a month to consider the person's fitness for the office and to offer private feedback to the elders. All of this occurs before the congregation formally votes to install the person into the diaconate.

Different churches will test deacon candidates differently. That's fine. The above process has worked well within our church's elder-led congregationalist polity, but what matters most is that your church has *some* means of vetting the character and competence of potential deacons—before it's too late. Paul includes this qualification to protect the precious body of Christ.

6. Faithful Family Life

Paul's final requirement is that a deacon's godliness must extend to his closest relationships. No, that's wrong: it must *begin* with his closest relationships.

If a man is married, he must love his wife and be faithful to her alone—a one-woman man.[8] Your church can always get another deacon, but a deacon's wife can't get another husband. Serving one's spouse is the ultimate training ground for serving the saints.

If the deacon has children, he must raise them in an atmosphere of gentle firmness and joyful love, establishing not

---

[8] Is divorce in a person's past an automatic, permanent disqualifier from holding diaconal office? I'm not convinced it is. The "one-woman man" qualification is about faithfulness to one's present spouse. What is the person's reputation now? Can he be held up as a model for faithfully following Christ? Nor do I believe that single Christians, whether never-married or widowed, are inherently disqualified. "One-woman man" refers to unquestioned chastity in all of one's relationships.

only the beliefs but the morale of his home. In a word, he must manage his family with deliberateness and diligence, thereby training his heart to serve the church in the same manner.

The apostle could not be clearer: there is no such thing as a good deacon who is a lousy husband or dad. Being a "good family man" is not a bonus in considering someone for the diaconate; it is a prerequisite.

THE PROMISE

Before leaving the subject of deacons, Paul emphasizes one more critical point. He knows that deaconing is not for the faint of heart. Much of it is thankless—grunt work, not stage work. So what will keep a deacon going amid exhaustion and discouragement? A promise:

> For those who serve well as deacons gain a good standing for themselves and also great confidence in the faith that is in Christ Jesus. (1 Tim. 3:13)

A faithful deacon will receive two gifts in increasing measure: respect and boldness. The first comes horizontally from the church; the other descends vertically from God. Given the "downward" shape of diaconal work, this promise of respect is particularly beautiful, isn't it? Though the call to diaconal service is not glamorous, the reward is glorious. In the meantime, Paul's charge in Galatians 6:9 applies to every deacon: "Let us not grow weary of doing good, for in due season we will reap, if we do not give up."

Do the deacons in your church feel respected? Do they know how much you appreciate their service? Before you turn to the next chapter, take a moment to encourage a deacon in your church. Give them a call. Buy them a gift card. Offer to babysit their kids. Send them an email. Just do something to put wind in their sails—"a word in season, how good it is!" (Prov. 15:23; cf. 25:11; 16:24). Such encouragements are for the good of the flock and the glory of God.

HAVEN'T WE HEARD THIS BEFORE?

I find it interesting that Paul's standards for deacons don't represent the first time the Ephesian church (where Timothy was serving) had heard about these themes. The thematic parallels between his more general letter to members of the Ephesian church, written around AD 60, and the qualifications for deacons listed in 1 Timothy 3:8–13, written around AD 62–64, are striking.

A deacon must . . .	Ephesians
Not be double-tongued	4:29
Not be addicted to much wine	5:18
Not be greedy for dishonest gain	4:28; 5:5
Hold the mystery of the faith	3:1–10
Be faithful in marriage	5:22–33
Manage his children well	6:1–4

A deacon will . . .	
Gain confidence in the faith	6:19

Why is this significant? Just consider what it reveals. It shows that, above all else, a deacon must simply be a faithful Christian. Theologian D. A. Carson has noted that what's most extraordinary about the qualifications for elders (1 Tim. 3:1–7; Titus 1:6–9) is just how ordinary they are. The same observation applies to the qualifications for deacons—only more so, since a deacon need not be "able to teach" like an elder (1 Tim. 3:2).

The standards in 1 Timothy 3:8–13 sound a nonnegotiable note: deacons must embody the kind of character expected of all Christians. But they should be exemplary in the ordinary. Deacons are the people in your church of whom you should be able to say, "Brother, do you desire to foster unity? Sister, do you wish to grow as a servant? Watch *them*."

NO BETTER METRIC

The saints of Middletown Community Church are rightly thankful for Leroy's business acumen, Shelby's generosity, Keith's knack for fixing stuff, Alex's longevity, and Juan's desire to serve as an elder.

All of these descriptors are good things in the life of a church—but, as we saw earlier, none of them, taken alone, qualifies anyone to serve as a deacon. To determine fitness for the office of deacon, the congregation will need to measure each candidate's life against the only God-breathed metric: 1 Timothy 3:8–13.

4

THE BREAKDOWN: WHAT DEACONS MUST DO

Nick became a deacon three years ago, and he wears it like a badge of honor. Yes, he's quick to mutter "glory to God" for any recognition he receives, but it sure seems as if his identity as a church member—maybe even his identity as a Christian— is wrapped up in his position as a deacon. Consequently, he's not very flexible. Once Nick gets an idea, the armies of heaven should be prepared to stand down. He's not some ordinary lay-man, after all. He's a *deacon*.

Bill was installed as a deacon when the senior pastor, Chase, was in kindergarten. With twenty-seven years of service under his belt, Bill is not about to let some well-meaning whip-persnapper waltz in and "re-envision" his role. *I don't doubt he learned some interesting things in seminary*, Bill thinks, *but this is the real world. I've been serving this church longer than Chase has been able to spell "deacon." If he doesn't like the way we do things here, he's welcome to find another church.*

Craig has served as deacon chairman for ten years and is beloved by all. Early in his tenure he deftly navigated consecutive budget shortfalls that almost sank the church. Craig has both gravitas and clout. Whenever he speaks, two things happen: people listen and stuff gets done. In recent months, Pastor Ryan has begun teaching on the topic of church leadership, and it has ruffled some feathers. Apparently he attended a weekend conference, read a couple books, and now wants to demote deacons. Or at least that's how it seems. What else could all this talk of "installing elders" mean? Craig, though, doesn't share his fellow deacons' angst. *Brothers*, he says, *we have long served this church, and done so faithfully, but that doesn't mean we have nothing to learn. When was the last time we actually studied what the Scriptures teach about deacons? I think we should hear Pastor Ryan out.*

JOB DESCRIPTION

The previous two chapters focused on what a deacon should *be*. We saw that character, not a set of life skills, is paramount. But character is not everything. Deacons are not installed to have quiet times, after all; they are charged to perform tasks.

Let's explore in greater detail what a deacon is meant to *do*. At the broadest level, I believe diaconal work encompasses three things in the life of a church.

1. Spotting and Meeting Tangible Needs

A church without biblically functioning deacons will be perpetually distracted from its central mission of making disciples (Matt. 28:18–20). This was the apparent impetus behind the apostles' decision to establish the seven in Acts 6: inequitable food distribution had evoked a serious complaint and exposed a sensitive fault line in the church. Resolving the tension was important, even urgent. Yet the apostles had both the conviction and the wherewithal to detect an even greater threat: tackling every short-term problem themselves would only pave the way for long-term disaster. Neglecting the ministry of teaching and prayer would eventually gut the very heart of the church.

So the apostles led the congregation in setting apart seven men, known for their godliness and wisdom, who would coordinate a solution. Informed by this precedent, diaconal work through the centuries has focused chiefly on tangible needs, particularly caring for the poor and vulnerable. Indeed, diaconal work should never involve *less* than such benevolence care or mercy ministry. The larger principle of the deacon's role, though, includes anything in a church's life that threatens to distract and derail elders from their primary responsibilities.

All of this suggests that a deacon should be skilled at spotting practical needs and then taking the initiative to meet them efficiently. But the best deacons don't just *react* to present problems; they also *anticipate* future ones.[1] They love to brainstorm creative solutions to anything that might potentially impede the work of the elders and the flourishing of the Word.

Biblical deacons, then, are like a congregation's offensive linemen, whose job is to protect the quarterback. They rarely

---

[1] As William Godfrey puts it, "The diaconate ought not be content to concern themselves only with those obvious needs which drop into their laps. . . . Deacons who do not spend time getting to know the members of the congregation will have no hope of discovering the needs which require their attention and intervention. Thus, the ministry of deacons . . . must be proactive" (William Godfrey, "Getting Acquainted with the Congregation's Needs," in *Faithful and Fruitful: Essays for Elders and Deacons*, ed. William Boekestein and Steven Swets [Middleville, MI: Reformed Fellowship, 2019], 138, 139).

get attention, much less credit, but their labors are utterly indispensable for both guarding and advancing the ministry of the Word. Without effective deacons, elders will suffer incessant distraction and get sacked by an onrush of practical demands.

Pastor, when eyeing future deacons, look for godly saints who see and meet needs discreetly (they don't need or want credit), at their own expense (they sacrifice), and without being asked (they take the initiative to solve problems).[2] Warning signs in a deacon candidate, then, will include not merely a tendency to be quarrelsome but also a tendency to be disorganized or unreliable. This is why I said above that character, though it is the main thing, is not quite everything. A godly member who regularly flakes out, or never returns emails, or always needs to be told what to do, is not yet a good fit for the office. A deacon must be reliable, neither angling for authority nor needing to be babysat. In essence, a deacon should be "a safe pair of hands."

Show me a church with distracted pastors and a derailed mission, and I will show you a church without effective deacons.

2. Protecting and Promoting Church Unity

The diaconate is designed to safeguard the harmony of the church. Just as the seven were tasked to salvage the unity of the Jerusalem church, so deacons today (as we have seen) are meant to play a pivotal role as "shock absorbers" in congregational life.

A contentious Christian, therefore, will make a poor deacon. So what *should* mark a deacon? Palpable humility. A spirit

---

[2] I am indebted to Jeff Wiesner for this wording.

of gentleness. A willingness to be flexible. The ability to stand on conviction without being combative.

One way to discern if a deacon candidate is "wired" for the role is simply to consider whether their reflection is easily seen in verses like the following:

- *"Blessed are the peacemakers, for they shall be called sons of God"* (Matt. 5:9). Note that Jesus commends peacemakers, not mere peacekeepers. It isn't enough to simply refrain from strife; indeed, this may even indicate a debilitating fear of man. Instead, Proverbs teaches us that "those who plan peace have joy" (Prov. 12:20). Deacon, do you merely affirm the beauty of peace, or do you *plan* it? Would others describe you as someone who "seeks peace and pursues it" (Ps. 34:14)?

- *"Good sense makes one slow to anger, and it is his glory to over-look an offense"* (Prov. 19:11). Deacon, are you able to let things go? Does self-control mark your responses to the in-evitable disagreements you have with others? I'm not talk-ing about the authority of Scripture or the deity of Christ. I'm talking about more minor matters, things on which rea-sonable minds can differ. Or are you inclined to treat every issue like it's an ecclesial emergency?

- *"I appeal to you, brothers, by the name of our Lord Jesus Christ, that all of you agree, and that there be no divisions among you, but that you be united in the same mind and the same judgment. For it has been reported to me by Chloe's peo-ple that there is quarreling among you, my brothers"* (1 Cor. 1:10–11). As examples to the flock, deacons should be especially slow to perpetuate any kind of partisan spirit. Satan loves to watch factionalism expand its tentacles and slowly suffocate a church. Deacon, are you alert to his schemes (2 Cor. 2:11)? Avoiding divisiveness yourself is good; anticipating and thwarting it in others is even better.

- *"I entreat Euodia and I entreat Syntyche to agree in the Lord"* (Phil. 4:2). This verse, like the others, certainly isn't addressed to deacons only. And yet a congregation's deacons should be among the first to model this kind of *let's agree* impulse. To be clear, this call to agreement is not about sameness. The point is not to suppress who God has made you to be or to never voice your opinion or to avoid all disagreement or to essentially foster a congregation of clones. That's called *uniformity*, and it's the essence of cults. What marks healthy churches is *unity*, which is both messier and more beautiful than mere sameness. Deacons must be on the front lines of facilitating this kind of hard-won agreement in the Lord.

A final passage to ponder is 1 Corinthians 13. This famous "love chapter" doesn't exist because Paul misfiled an old wedding sermon. It's not designed to make a starry-eyed couple feel gooey, but to make a divided church feel ashamed. If you're a deacon, here's a challenge: revisit 1 Corinthians 13 soon. Read it slowly and honestly consider how your life these days—including your demeanor as a deacon—measures up. But don't stop there. Find someone who knows you well—ideally a leader in your church—and invite their honest assessment. Where do they see your conduct and attitude reflecting the love described in 1 Corinthians 13? Where do they struggle to see the reflection?

The kind of love that's worth anything, Paul says, "bears all things, believes all things, hopes all things, endures all things" (1 Cor. 13:7). Are you on the front lines, deacon, of encouraging your fellow church members to assume the best of one another, to give the benefit of the doubt, to be easy to please and hard to offend?

Consider Mark Dever's insight here:

> You don't want people serving as deacons who are unhappy with your church. The deacons should never be the ones who complain the loudest or jar the church with their actions or attitudes. Quite the opposite! . . . You don't want to nominate deacons who don't recognize the importance of the ministry of preaching and teaching, but people who are anxious to protect it. More broadly, you want the most supportive people in the church to serve as the deacons. So when you're considering who might serve as a deacon, look for people with gifts of encouragement.[3]

A qualified deacon will increasingly resemble the kind of unity-forging love the Bible so clearly commands.

3. Serving and Supporting the Ministry of the Elders

One of my favorite television shows is *The West Wing*, an early-2000s political drama that chronicles life in the White House. Throughout the seven-season series there is a phrase, almost a mantra, that resounds from various characters: "I serve at the pleasure of the president."

Likewise, godly deacons in a healthy church will increasingly say, "We serve at the pleasure of the elders." This language is not authoritarian, for just as the American president is finally accountable to the American people, so a church's

---

[3] Mark Dever, *Understanding Church Leadership*, Church Basics, ed. Jonathan Leeman (Nashville: B&H, 2016), 13, 14.

elders are finally accountable to the church's members. (And even more fundamentally, of course, the elders serve at the pleasure of King Jesus.) Nevertheless, Jesus has embedded different layers of life-giving authority into his church. Deacons serve at the elders' pleasure not because elders are ultimate, but because Jesus is. And this is how, in immeasurable wisdom, he has designed his church to function.

Along these lines Alexander Strauch has argued, I think persuasively, that deacons are best understood as "formal assistants to the elders."[4]

Before I proceed, I should acknowledge that not all churches have elders. In many cases, the deacon board may function in an elder-like capacity. If that's how your church is structured, may I challenge you in two ways? First, consider afresh the biblical case for elders as a separate office, devoted to oversight and teaching. Elders are not, as some might suppose, just a "Presbyterian thing." They are a biblical thing. And I believe the case for this distinct office is convincing.[5]

Second, regardless of where you presently land on the issue of elders, don't give up on this book. Don't let the language of "elders" distract you from the Bible's instruction about deacons. When I say deacons should serve as *assistants to the elders*, in some churches that will be exemplified, at least for the time being, as *assistants to the staff pastors*. That's fine. Yet to the de-

---

[4] Alexander Strauch, *Paul's Vision for the Deacons* (Colorado Springs: Lewis & Roth, 2017). See chapter 3 ("Deacons, Assistants to the Elders") in particular.

[5] Again, see Jeramie Rinne, *Church Elders: How to Shepherd God's People Like Jesus* (Wheaton, IL: Crossway, 2014). For those in solo-pastor/board-of-deacons churches wanting to know why and how to move to a plurality of elders, see Phil Newton and Matt Schmucker, *Elders in the Life of the Church: Rediscovering the Biblical Model for Church Leadership*, rev. ed. (Grand Rapids, MI: Kregel, 2014).

gree that your deacons function as pseudo-elders, your need to rethink that model in light of Scripture is all the more urgent, for a simple reason: when deacons function as elders, who will function as deacons? In such arrangements, the congregation misses out on the blessing of *both* offices as delineated in God's Word.

Alright, parenthesis closed. Back to our premise of deacons as "formal assistants to the elders." Strauch's latest book on the diaconate, *Paul's Vision for the Deacons*, is an essential resource defending this view. He marshals a number of salient points; I will mention three.

The first is a bit technical, but here it is: the *diakon-* ["deacon"] word group isn't always related to the idea of table service. It can express agency at the behest of a superior. Indeed, this is how the first entry in the leading Greek-English lexicon (popularly known as BDAG) renders it. Channeling the groundbreaking work of Clarence D. Agan III,[6] Strauch notes, "In recent years scholars have shown that there is a wider linguistic range of meaning of the *diakon-* word group than previously acknowledged." It is not limited to connotations of menial labor or table service, in other words. "In many contexts," Strauch writes, "the idea is that of a subordinate carrying out an assignment on a superior's behalf and having full authority to execute the superior's delegated task."[7]

---

[6] Clarence D. Agan III, "Like the One Who Serves: Jesus, Servant-Likeness, and Self-Humiliation in the Gospel of Luke" (PhD dissertation, University of Aberdeen, 1999).
[7] Strauch, *Paul's Vision for the Deacons*, 53–54. Strauch adds a noteworthy detail: "[T]he third edition of *A Greek-English Lexicon of the New Testament and Other Early Christian Literature* (abbreviated as *BDAG*), following more recent research on the *diakon-* word group, lists one entry for the Greek word *diakonos* as: 'one who gets something done, at the behest of a superior, *assistant* to someone.' The entries for *diakonos* as it appears in Philippians 1:1 and 1 Timothy 3:8, 12 are '*attendant, assistant, aide*'" (54). A number of scholars now affirm this view; Strauch lists twenty examples (64–65n1).

Along these lines, second, there is nothing in the context of 1 Timothy 3 to suggest—much less demand—that deacons solely function as table-serving officials who care for the poor. Even in Acts 6, where this idea is plainly present, the seven are serving at the apostles' behest. Surely the most natural implication, then, is not that diaconal focus is *limited* to mercy ministry, just that it's not *less* than mercy ministry. Plenty of other needs can arise which impede the elders' ministry of the Word and prayer and therefore demand the attention of deacons.

Third, it is noteworthy and not accidental that Paul turns his attention to deacons (1 Tim. 3:8–12) immediately after discussing elders (1 Tim. 3:1–7). It's as if he doesn't want us to catch our breath lest we miss the inseparable connection— even the logical order—between the two offices. The structure of the passage suggests that deacons are both paired with and subordinate to the elders they support. "The deacons are not a separate, autonomous body of officials disconnected from the body of overseers," Strauch observes. "As the context and the terms themselves indicate, the *diakonoi* [deacons] operate under the leadership of the *episkopoi* [overseers]. The *diakonoi* assist the *episkopoi* by officially representing the overseers and standing ready to carry out tasks delegated by the overseers."[8] This relationship between the offices is also implied in the other passage where deacons (plural) are mentioned:

---

[8] Strauch, *Paul's Vision for the Deacons*, 57. He concludes, "[T]he assistants-to-the-overseers view is the best interpretation because it provides the most objective evidence both lexically and contextually with the least amount of guesswork involved. Furthermore, I am persuaded that the assistant-to-the-overseers view is the best option because the alternative views are unsatisfactory, demand too much guesswork, and cannot ultimately be proven contextually or lexically. So much of what I hear and read about deacons is based on mere assertion rather than evidence or argumentation" (63).

Paul and Timothy, servants of Christ Jesus,

To all the saints in Christ Jesus who are at Philippi, with the overseers and deacons. (Phil. 1:1)

The purpose of deacons is inseparably tied to the priority of elders.

The late Presbyterian theologian Edmund Clowney observes: "The account of Acts 6, and the broad use of *diakonos* in the letters, has therefore led to the conclusion that deacons are assistants to the ministers of the Word, rather than officers charged specifically with the ministry of mercy."[9]

This, by the way, is why it is misguided when deacons function as a separate power bloc or second house of the legislature through which bills need to be passed. Dever offers a helpful illustration:

> If the elders say, "Let's drive to Pittsburgh," it's not up to the deacons to come back and say, "No, let's drive to Philadelphia instead." They can legitimately come back and say, "Our engine won't get us to Pittsburgh. Perhaps we should reconsider." That's very helpful. But in general their job is to support the destination set by the elders.[10]

The elders of a church are not infallible—far from it. Nevertheless, insofar as we are looking to the Bible as our guide for church governance, deacons are never presented as chaperones of the elders who impose a potential "check" on their

---

[9] Edmund P. Clowney, *The Church*, Contours of Christian Theology (Downers Grove, IL: IVP Academic, 1995), 213.
[10] Dever, *Understanding Church Leadership*, 33.

every decision. In a healthy church, godly deacons execute the vision and oversight of godly elders, not the other way around.

TWO KEY DIFFERENCES

As we noted in the previous chapter, the qualifications for elders and deacons in 1 Timothy 3 are strikingly similar. So similar, in fact, that it seems Paul wants to draw our attention to the key difference: elders must be "able to teach" (1 Tim. 3:2; cf. Titus 1:9). This doesn't mean deacons may not teach, much less that they be unable to teach. (Remember Stephen and Philip!) It simply implies that the gift and responsibility of teaching is not a prerequisite for the office of deacon.

Also relevant is the fact that deacons are nowhere in the New Testament described as overseers or rulers. They will unavoidably exercise influence and a measure of natural leadership within a congregation, particularly in their areas of responsibility. No doubt the seven in Jerusalem had to organize, make decisions, delegate, and "lead" the relevant individuals in the distribution of food. If elders serve by leading, deacons lead by serving.[11] Nonetheless, deacons are never presented as spiritually authoritative leaders over the *whole* congregation. Elders alone are identified by their calling to exercise oversight (Acts 20:28; 1 Tim. 3:1–2; 5:17; 1 Pet. 5:2; Heb. 13:17). Members, likewise, are called to emulate deacons; they are never told to obey them.

---

[11] This phrasing is found both in H. B. Charles Jr., *On Pastoring: A Short Guide to Living, Leading, and Ministering as a Pastor* (Chicago: Moody, 2015), 88; and in Curtis C. Thomas, *Words of Encouragement and Counsel for a Lifetime of Ministry* (Wheaton, IL: Crossway, 2001), 106.

This is emphatically not to say that elders do ministry and deacons do not. On the contrary, the task of elders is to "equip the saints"—the whole congregation!—"for the work of ministry" (Eph. 4:12). The members are responsible for the mission. In terms of emphases, though, Jamie Dunlop's framework is helpful:

- Elders lead ministry.
- Deacons facilitate ministry.
- The congregation does ministry.[12]

Meeting tangible needs, promoting church unity, and assisting the elders—three broad parameters for diaconal service, beneath which lies much room for flexibility in application.

HEALTHY MODELS TODAY

We have established that deacons assist elders by coordinating acts of service, meeting tangible needs, and safeguarding church unity. It's time to get even more practical, though. How should a church's deacons actually function? How can they be organized and deployed in the best possible way?

There is no single healthy model for organizing deacons, but I will highlight three. Note the significant overlap between them.

1. Mercy Ministers

As we saw in chapter 1, and based largely on the precedent in Acts 6, the chief purpose of deacons throughout church history

---

[12] Jamie Dunlop, "Deacons: Shock Absorbers and Servants," *9Marks Journal*, Spring 2010. Since my church espouses elder-led congregationalism, we sometimes describe our polity in shorthand as "elder-led, deacon-served, congregation-ruled."

has been to care for the poor and needy, especially within the church. This focus has always been paramount, for example, in the Presbyterian and Reformed tradition. Tim Keller, who served as director of mercy ministries for the Presbyterian Church in America (PCA) before pastoring in Manhattan, asks, "What does a deacon do? He ministers in the name of Jesus among lonely, sick, elderly, orphaned, widowed, dying, poor, and deprived people."[13]

Likewise, in a recent work Cornelis Van Dam contends that deacons are "charged with the ministry of mercy to show the love of Christ by providing for the poor and afflicted."[14] In caring for the needs of the poor, deacons remove barriers to congregational joy. Central to a deacon's duty, Van Dam explains, is "the responsibility to ensure that the joy of redemption is shared by all," which entails "making certain that the poor and needy are helped and that no one lives uncomforted in the communion of saints."[15]

Biblical mercy ministry should be directed primarily toward those suffering within the church family, though not exclusively so (Gal. 6:10). Caring for the disadvantaged and distressed outside the church can be a powerful catalyst for proclaiming Christ's grace and demonstrating his love. Indeed, much discussion in recent years has centered around the role

---

[13] Timothy J. Keller, *Resources for Deacons: Love Expressed through Mercy Ministries* (Lawrenceville, GA: Presbyterian Church in America Committee on Discipleship Ministries, 1985), 11. It's important to note that the Presbyterian and Reformed tradition does not limit diaconal work to mercy ministry. In the same resource, Keller lists four categories of diaconal work: mercy, stewardship, property, and helps (30).

[14] Cornelis Van Dam, *The Deacon: Biblical Foundations for Today's Ministry of Mercy* (Grand Rapids, MI: Reformation Heritage, 2016), xi.

[15] Van Dam, *The Deacon*, 76.

of "social action" in the mission of the church: Is the church's mission to preach the gospel, to care for the poor, some combination of the two, or something else entirely? These are important conversations, and they hinge on important distinctions—for instance, whether by "church" you're referring to the *institution* or to the *individuals*.

In my estimation, though, much confusion would be alleviated by attending more carefully to this age-old feature of diaconal ministry. Scripture is clear that the central mission of the church is not to cure global poverty, but to preach gospel grace; it's not to transform the world, but to make disciples heralding the One who *has* (Matt. 28:18–20; cf. Acts 1:8). But this by no means suggests that the work of a church is exclusively spiritual. This whole book is about a formal office God established in his church for the sake of giving practical help to those who need it most. Again, diaconal work is more than mercy ministry, but it is not less.

I sometimes perceive an ironic similarity between churches who want to "just preach the gospel" and those who want to "transform the culture." The one tends to oppose social ministry in favor of gospel proclamation; the other tends to champion social ministry instead of gospel proclamation. Yet both are susceptible to an impoverished view of the diaconate. In "just preach the gospel" churches, diaconal mercy ministry can be seen as unimportant; in "transform the culture" churches, diaconal mercy ministry can be seen as superfluous and unnecessary—for it's what the whole congregation exists to do already. In the former, the mission of the church manages to downplay this diaconal role; in the latter, this calling of deacons *becomes* the mission of the church.

Thus it is crucial, in healthy churches rightly committed to preaching Christ and making disciples, that we not diminish the diaconate—God's "social" office for catalyzing spiritual mission. Yes, it is true that the gospel would not have spread in Acts 6 had the apostles neglected their chief calling to preach and pray. But it's also true that the gospel likely would not have spread had the seven not risen to meet the widows' needs.

Perhaps today's highly charged conversations about the church's mission would move forward if we had some of these historic ecclesial categories more firmly in place. As we've seen, a holistic ministry that weds these concerns—gospel proclamation and gospel demonstration—is not the latest fad; it has been par for the course throughout church history. Deed ministry (diaconal) has always served Word ministry (pastoral). What God has joined together, let no church separate.

2. A Team of Leading Servants

In some churches, deacons meet as a deliberative body, in service to the elders, in order to generate ideas and coordinate plans for addressing administrative concerns. Gathering as a group can provide a healthy measure of synergy, camaraderie, and accountability.

Brian Croft, director of a ministry called Practical Shepherding, practiced such a model when he was a pastor. The deacons in his church met while Croft and his fellow elders met—simultaneously yet separately. Croft then had a follow-up meeting with the chairman of the deacons, and they both swapped relevant information. This included any matters the deacons believed the elders should be aware of, and vice versa. Often these discussions centered on areas of overlap—things for which both groups were, in some measure, responsible.

Imagine, for example, a deacon is serving an elderly saint at her house. No matter how many appliances he fixes, if he leaves without inquiring how she's doing spiritually and praying with her, he has fallen short. Likewise, if an elder is at her house to care for her soul, but doesn't offer to move the heavy table, *he* has failed. While a division of labor between the offices is important, the deeds of each are not mutually exclusive. Elders, despite their spiritual focus, should remain practically aware. Deacons, despite their practical focus, should remain spiritually aware.

If you're a deacon, I hope it's clear that you have been called to far more than a monthly meeting. Deaconing is not an extracurricular activity for your spiritual résumé. It is the means by which your Savior has chosen to use you, in this season of your life, to serve the church he bought with his blood. In light of his mercy, I urge you to give yourself afresh to your diaconal work.

3. Role-Specific Ministry Mobilizers

In my own church, we have role-specific diaconal positions. Rather than meeting as a deliberative body, deacons are elected to specific diaconates and are encouraged to coordinate volunteer teams as needs arise. Currently we have fourteen different diaconates, though the number fluctuates in response to congregational needs. Just last month, for instance, we dissolved our diaconate of missionary care after concluding that one of our staff pastors could manage the responsibilities more seamlessly and without too much strain. Here are some common diaconal tasks listed in our church's constitution:

- Seeing that the sick, the sorrowing, the aged, and the infirm receive spiritual and physical comfort;
- Leading the hospitality ministries of the church;
- Attending to the normal care and maintenance of church properties;
- Receiving, holding, and disbursing a fund for benevolence, and reporting from time to time on the use of such funds to both the elders and the church;
- Attending to the accommodations for public worship;
- Assisting in distributing the elements during the Lord's Supper; and
- Serving in other specific capacities as the church has need.[16]

Note both the specificity in this list as well as the extraordinary measure of latitude afforded by the final line.

Some may dismiss such a model. Perhaps, say, a "deacon of parking" seems rather ridiculous. I can understand the logic: *If parking demands a deacon position, what doesn't?* But think about this for a moment. Parking is one of the most crucial logistical matters in the life of a church because it directly affects the most basic thing the church does: gather together. If people struggle to find parking, the gathering is impeded; and if the gathering is impeded, the very essence of the church—

---

[16] Third Avenue Baptist Church Constitution, article 3 ("Government"), section 5, clauses 7–13. Available at www.thirdavenue.org.

God's saints bound by his ordinances and assembled under his Word—may be threatened. One church I know in a crowded downtown area had only a few parking spots for its hundreds of members. The elders caught wind that members would sometimes get into arguments over those spots on Sunday morning. Therefore, they recommended that the church establish a deacon of parking both to tackle the tangible need and also to address a point of disunity in the life of the body.

WORKING TOGETHER

In his article "Deacons: Shock Absorbers and Servants," Jamie Dunlop raises a legitimate dilemma: How do we encourage deacons to be entrepreneurial unity-builders who do not encroach on the elders' leadership of the church, and so cause disunity? Dunlop's church also has role-specific diaconal positions, and his counsel is worth quoting at length:

> **Deacon Meetings:** If the goal of deacons is to support the directional decisions made by the elders, then deacons do not need to meet as a deliberative body—especially if your deacons each facilitate ministry in one specific area, such as childcare or hospitality (as they do in my church). Certainly there is no biblical model of deacons "sharing power" with elders, as do the House and Senate in the U.S. legislature.

> **Committees:** When standing diaconal committees begin to feel that they "own" specific ministry areas of the church, it becomes difficult for them to *avoid* making direction-setting decisions that should be left to the elders. After all, even things as "worldly" as the building or the budget have highly spiritual dimensions in their administration. As such, churches should

consider making any committees task-focused and time-limited, chartered to complete a task assigned by the elders.

Communication: Most diaconal ministries will at least occasionally run up against direction-level decisions that need to go to the elders. At our church we have found it useful to assign each deacon to an elder who regularly communicates what the elders are deciding in their meetings. The elders can then take direction-level issues in the deacon's work back to the larger body of elders as needed.[17]

Whichever practical model your church favors, the most important thing is that the role of deacons is biblically understood. This clarity provides an essential foundation for diaconal ministry.[18]

Finally, it's crucial to emphasize that the most effective deacons don't do everything themselves. They are mobilizers. Note how Van Dam concludes his reflections on Acts 6: "We may therefore assume that the seven did not personally do the distributing but would have played a coordinating, helping, and overseeing role to ensure none was bypassed."[19] Earlier I mentioned that good deacons don't need to be babysat. They can be trusted and relied upon to both execute and expand their sphere of service without

---

[17] Dunlop, "Deacons: Shock Absorbers and Servants," emphasis original.

[18] A church's documents (specifically its constitution and bylaws) can play a key role in clarifying parameters for how elders/pastors and deacons operate—and how they're expected to relate in terms of responsibility. Invigorating both offices according to Scripture requires more than clear documents, of course, but rarely does it involve less. As a practical example, I do not believe a church's bylaws should specify how many deacons it must have, since this can result in pressing unqualified people into service to get the required number. It is wiser, I think, to leave the number open.

[19] Van Dam, *The Deacon*, 59.

constant supervision or correction. So, as you scan your church for qualified deacons, don't just look for work-horses. Look for those who will faithfully *organize* service, not simply do it all themselves.

WHAT DOES THE BOOK SAY?

Remember Craig, the chairman who encouraged his disgruntled deacons to hear out their young pastor, Ryan, on the topic of church leadership? It was the right move—but why? Well, not because Pastor Ryan necessarily had it all figured out (he may not have). Nor because deacons must check their brains at the door (they shouldn't) since they are mere handymen (they aren't). Nor because deacons have no right to register disagreement with their pastor or elders (they do). The reason this was the right move is because God's people—from the oldest leader to newest believer—should always be open to revisiting assumptions and revising practices in light of God's Word.

In Acts 17, Paul and Silas flee persecution in Thessalonica and stumble into Berea, where they enter a synagogue and begin proclaiming Jesus as the Messiah. How does the audience respond?

> Now the Berean Jews were of more noble character than those in Thessalonica, for they received the message with great eagerness and examined the Scriptures every day to see if what Paul said was true. (Acts 17:11 NIV)

The Bereans aren't listening mindlessly; they're checking Paul's teaching against the Hebrew Scriptures. Luke doesn't rebuke them for not taking an apostle at his word; he *commends* them. This is extraordinary.

Again, what matters most is not how we prefer to think about deacons, nor how our church has always "done" them, nor what this book says about them. What finally matters is what *God* has revealed. Church tradition has its important place in the life of a congregation, but when it comes to your job description for deacons, be sure you're pulling it from inerrant pages.

5

THE BENEFITS:
WHAT DEACONS PROVIDE

What does it actually look like, on the ground, when deacons function in the ways I've sought to outline in this book?

To help answer that question I canvassed scores of friends, both pastors and deacons, in search of simple stories that capture the purpose and beauty of diaconal work. Discussions about deacons—yes, books included—can sometimes seem a bit fuzzy, like watching an old VHS tape. So I hope this string of vignettes will further crystallize the biblical principles and practices we've examined. I hope it will feel like you're watching those principles and practices take on flesh, with richer color and sharper lines. I hope it will feel like you're reading in HD.

As you will notice, though, faithful diaconal service is not typically epic or extraordinary. At least, it doesn't appear that way to our fallen human eyes. But make no mistake: the power of Almighty God courses through the ministry of effective deacons. While their work may be quiet, even subtle, they are indispensable instruments in advancing the kingdom of Jesus Christ.[1]

THE STORIES

One of the best things we've done as a church is emphasize membership. Though we realize that no person will know everyone equally well, we want everyone to be equally known. That's our goal. We've even started to see some success.

As people become more known, though, needs rise to the surface. These needs—whether spiritual or material—can quickly stack up and overwhelm an elder body. Just as in Acts 6, it's incredibly hard to devote time to praying for the body, preparing messages for the body, and raising up leaders in the body while working through tactical, nitty-gritty details like helping a young mom facing a divorce or a member struggling to manage finances.

Our church's deacon of member care has truly been a gift from God. Both he and his wife have rolled up their sleeves and spent countless hours with members in need. If a member needs a little bit of money to get through the month, this deacon will do more than submit a request to the benevolence team; he'll meet with the member and try to get to the root of the problem. Are there spending patterns that need to be addressed? Is the person sufficiently plugged into the body to get help from members organically, without special intervention? Does the person simply need someone to provide budgeting or job-search counsel?

---

[1] Names have been changed or omitted for privacy; otherwise, all details are exactly as reported.

As time has gone on, I've come to realize there are several members who have been assisted by this deacon and his wife that I didn't even know about. Long story short, without our deacon of member care, hours and hours could be spent by elders in meetings or other efforts, trying to solve these problems. But this deacon and his team are amazing, truly ingrained in the life of the church, and this has freed me up as an elder to focus on my responsibilities of teaching and prayer. To top it off, hardly a month goes by without this couple graciously telling me how thankful they are for all I do. It's humbling and invigorating.

———

I was still a rookie: thirty-two years old and only a couple years into my first pastorate. One man in the church—a longstanding member who, though nice, regularly sowed seeds of discord—was trying to restore things to the ways of the "past," when committees ran the church. He also began talking to other members, asking if they thought I needed to grow as a preacher.

Things escalated when he turned those conversations into a "list" of likeminded objectors which he planned to present at a business meeting, almost like a petition. I felt like I was in a tough spot: on the one hand, I always desire to improve in preaching; yet on the other hand, I knew I couldn't really fight that battle.

Our lead deacon at the time caught wind of the list and sprang into action. He assured me of his support, got ahold of the list, and proceeded to call the first five people on it. He asked what their concerns were and if they had issues with me; then he asked why they hadn't directed the criticism to me personally instead of joining a grumbling group. These members were actually horrified they were on a "list"—they didn't even know it existed. This deacon then called the man and told him that undermining the pastor was hurting the church, and that he needed to stop and find a healthier, more biblical way to express his opinions. As it turned out, most of the folks on the list ended up communicating to me their trust and support, rather than anything discouraging. The situation was totally defused because one deacon had the wherewithal—and courage—to rise up and address a situation I couldn't. He protected the unity of the church at a pivotal moment. I'm now in year thirteen, and I honestly think surviving years two and three would have been almost impossible without that deacon's support.

———

Our church in Iraq has members from across the world. When Freddie returned home to India to attend his father's funeral, he was astonished by the number of folks who shared that his dad, who had been an elder in his church, had served them. This not only encouraged Freddie but caused him to reexamine his own life. Back in Iraq, despite working for an aid and relief organization, Freddie was dissatisfied that he wasn't better serving people in his church. *If I died,* he thought, *no one would show up at my funeral and tell the kind of stories I heard at my dad's.*

At this time, the regional humanitarian crisis was flaring up and our church was regularly receiving impoverished visitors—whether international refugees or native, internally displaced Iraqis whose homes had been destroyed by ISIS. We desperately needed an Acts 6 deacon of benevolence.

Freddie, who met the biblical qualifications and desired to serve, was soon nominated to the church and installed into the role. He immediately began working with the elders to draft a benevolence policy. Prior to this, the elders had been making every benevolence decision—which involved tracking people down and having a range of conversations to discern credibility, set parameters, distribute funds, offer ongoing accountability and support, and so on. This was important work, of course, but it was consuming the elders' time. It is not an overstatement to say that Freddie's diaconal service relieved an enormous burden from the elders, met a pressing need in the church, and, in the process, transformed his own life.

———

When I became pastor here over ten years ago, we had a homeless man in our congregation. He would faithfully show up for worship, and also for a disability support group during the week. Depending on the time of year, he might stay at the Salvation Army shelter, or couch surf around town, walking wherever he went. Then I found him sleeping in one of our Sunday school rooms, beside a box with some of his belongings.

This led to quite a few conversations, from which I learned that he struggled with alcohol abuse, drug abuse, depression, bipolar disorder, and that he had suffered both physical and sexual abuse as a child. God had saved him and given him a tender heart for serving the downtrodden and outcasts of our community. By the grace of God, he eventually obtained stable housing, a vehicle, and part-time work. Although at times he has been suicidal and admitted to the local crisis center, through all of his struggles he has sacrificed himself to serve others in our congregation.

Because of his love for Scripture, and eagerness to serve those with special needs, the elders recommended him as deacon for disability and general needs. He has taken upon himself the task of cutting grass, picking up litter, and emptying trash at the church property. But most of all, he seeks to serve those living with some of the struggles he has experienced. He has invited many to attend worship and to hear the gospel. And during worship, he can be found helping or encouraging someone who struggles with more disability than himself. What a blessing to the people of God he is!

———

I was a young pastor and the only elder, serving with a deacon board of eight. About a year into my pastorate, a deacon questioned a few decisions of the finance committee, which upset some ladies on it. Almost immediately their husbands started demanding this deacon's resignation—and pressuring me to make it happen.

Earl, a respected patriarch in his seventies, was serving as the chairman of the deacons. He took me to lunch and looked me in the eye: "Preacher, I don't know why people are saying what they're saying, but I want you to know I have your back. We're going to get through this. Let's pray." He then went to those men and stood in the gap, essentially taking the conflict for me. "We're going to let our pastor lead," he told them.

Had Deacon Earl not led the way in quelling that conflict, I doubt I would have survived here. I truly believe God used him to save my pastorate.

But this wasn't the only way Deacon Earl strategically served. It's no secret that change can be hard for those who've been in the same church for decades. When our church started attracting younger folks and everything that can bring with it—backward caps, noisy settings, and so on—he didn't fold his arms; he welcomed them with open arms. With his big mustache and even bigger smile, newcomers felt his warmth and love. Deacon Earl helped to turn the tide of our whole church.

Deacon Earl's death a couple years ago was one of the most bittersweet times in the life of our church, simply because of how beloved he was. He was a man who loved Jesus and couldn't wait to see him. And because he loved Jesus, he loved people. From the youngest to the oldest, everyone was affected by this conflict-solving, change-embracing, people-loving deacon.

———

As our church moved from a solo-pastor/deacon-board setup to a plurality of both elders and deacons, the first year of transition was challenging.[2] Even though the congregation and the deacons were in favor, it's not easy to move from a mindset of primarily decision makers to primarily servants. During this time a deacon named Dave was showing himself to be a natural and respected leader, so he became the chairman of the deacons.

Under Dave's gentle but firm leadership, the fundamental posture of the deacons shifted from "we need to hold our pastor accountable" to "we need to serve and support our elders." The goal wasn't, "How can we weigh in on all the decisions?" but "How can we make our elders' ministry easier?" Some of the deacons were slower to come around to this seemingly new concept; they were used to holding their thumb on the pastor when it came to decisions of finances, staff, and so forth. But one deacon was able to change the dynamic of the whole board.

I'll just say this: during a season of transition, it is invaluable to have a respected deacon leading change from within. Dave's eagerness to both lead the deacons and submit to the elders turned the tide of the whole deacon body, which in turn has produced all kinds of good fruit in our church. When I do pastoral visits now, it's rare that a deacon hasn't already been there, serving in strategic ways.

----

[2] For another example of a congregation moving to a plural-elder model, see Gregg Allison's account of chairing the board of deacons at Hinson Memorial Baptist Church in Portland, Oregon, shortly before the transition: Gregg Allison and Ryan Welsh, *Raising the Dust: "How-To" Equip Deacons to Serve the Church* (Louisville: Sojourn Network, 2019), 34–38.

It was a Sunday evening prayer service, and the senior pastor was spotlighting the ministry of a local crisis-pregnancy center. They had contacted our church: were any members able to meet with a couple who had decided to keep their unborn baby? My wife and I volunteered and met with Karla and her boyfriend several times; my wife and Karla became quite close, in fact. (The boyfriend ended up leaving the picture.) One of Karla's greatest needs was wise counsel—how in the world to raise a kid while working a job, arranging childcare, and attempting to stay sane. Amazingly, over the course of several months Karla's heart warmed to Jesus Christ; she became a believer, was baptized, and became a member of our church. Of course, this enabled my wife and me to connect her with even more brothers and sisters in the church. We got a front-row seat to watch her grow in faith. To be sure, none of this happened immediately: it was probably a full year from the time we met Karla to the moment she embraced Christ.

As one of our church's deacons for practical member care, I'll occasionally make a churchwide appeal: "If anyone desires to serve with us, or has extra resources you'd like to give to members in need, reach out and let us know." Well, a member contacted us to say that he was getting rid of a car and, rather than trading it in, wanted to donate it to someone in the church. I was thus able to connect Karla with this generous church member who didn't yet know her, and she got a good, working-condition vehicle for free.

It has been a privilege to walk with Karla through some of her darkest hours, especially early on. It certainly wasn't a quick fix, nor did we go it alone. I ran point as a deacon, yes, but the beautiful effort I got to spearhead was churchwide.

————

When Betty's husband started losing his mental faculties due to Parkinson's disease, she naturally felt overwhelmed, though she never complained. As a deacon, I reached out to recruit members to help her navigate this distressing stage of life. These folks served in droves, helping her move furniture, sift through piles of basement junk, and even pull off two yard sales. Gratefully, my job gave me the flexibility to visit Betty often, sometimes just to chat. (Deacons need not be gifted to teach, but they should be equipped to talk!) I also had the privilege of meeting her two daughters and sharing Christ with one of them. Betty faced a number of complicated financial decisions—from caring for her husband in his final months to making funeral arrangements to estimating personal health-care costs to, eventually, putting her house on the market. James 1:27 is clear: "Religion that is pure and undefiled before God the Father is this: to visit orphans and widows in their affliction, and to keep oneself unstained from the world." By God's grace, we were able to mobilize a James 1:27 ministry to Betty, reminding her often that she was not forgotten and was deeply loved.

All of this transpired, by the way, during a particularly tense season of racial unrest in America. Betty is an elderly white woman and I am a young black man; a friendship like ours might look strange, even scandalous, to a watching world.

But the blood that unites us runs deeper than anything that divides us. Indeed, anything is possible in Christ.

———

Here in Sevilla, Spain, one of our deacons organized and oversaw a ministry to our city's most impoverished neighborhoods. He recruited groups of church members to visit the area two evenings a month, and to seek out homeless persons or impoverished family units. The prayerful hope was to strike up gospel conversations while providing practical necessities like blankets, socks, and food.

One neighborhood in particular became deeply receptive to the gospel through the efforts of this deacon. Not only did they request a Bible study in their cardboard shacks, but some families began attending our worship services. At first we thought they might just be coming for giveaways; before long, however, people from that community were getting saved and baptized. In fact, a few months ago God enabled us to plant a gospel-preaching church in that neighborhood—an impossibility without the vision and initiative of one faithful deacon!

———

One Sunday at church, we noticed a young mom with kids sitting a few rows back. After the service, my wife introduced herself and learned that Trina had come to meet with one of my fellow deacons who oversees community care (a ministry providing practical needs and gospel witness to nonmembers). My wife got Trina's contact information and texted her later that week to invite her family over for dinner. In the meantime, we learned from the other deacon that Trina was facing several serious struggles; in fact, we went into dinner with no expectations about where the evening would lead. Sure enough, my wife pulled Trina aside: "Do you have a place to go with your kids tonight?" She admitted she didn't, so we encouraged her to stay with us and our children. Trina's family ended up living with us for several months, and now they live with another couple in the church. We don't think she's a believer yet, though we're grateful she's in a far more stable life situation than when she first walked through our church doors.

Of course, not every deacon is in a position to spontaneously host a struggling family for months on end. That's unreasonable. But our family was in a place where we felt we could handle it, with God's strength. Our church's ministry to Trina's family has been a coordinated effort, not a solo performance. Numerous members have shone when given the opportunity to serve.

Here's what I've learned as a deacon: to faithfully endure, you really must do everything as unto the Lord, not unto man (Col. 3:23). People can be frustrating to serve, after all. History's first diaconal job was to wade into a contentious situation and try to make sense of it (Acts 6). Deacons exist because of challenging situations! You are there to help bring peace amid tension and clarity amid complexity. Of course this isn't easy; it never has been. But the labor is worth it. So let us not grow weary, fellow deacons, in doing good. Our heavenly Father sees us, and service for him is never in vain (Gal. 6:9–10; 1 Cor. 15:58).

———

A godly woman in our church saw a gap in ministry and desired to coordinate a "helps ministry," very much akin to Acts 6. People came out of the woodwork to meet tangible needs and be part of the team. A list of homebound members was drawn up, and families were assigned to them to make weekly phone calls and regular visits. Those needing yard work, painting, and more were connected with those who could meet the need.

When a former elder died, his unbelieving adult daughter was overwhelmed by the physical condition of his estate. This diaconal "helps" team spearheaded a massive cleanup of his estate, providing a terrific gospel witness in the process.

This ministry also serves as the church's connection hub for organizing meals for members facing challenging times. And in the midst of the COVID-19 pandemic, it was the hub for matching all who needed help with those who wished to meet physical needs. The ministry remains a valuable way for the elders to keep even better tabs on the pulse of the church.

———

He's hard to miss in our congregation: bald head, earring, black leather pants. Hank was saved out of the drug culture, holds a high school diploma, and has worked manual labor jobs his whole life. He's also one of the most effective deacons I have ever known.

Hank and his wife arrived at the church I pastor about six months after my wife and I did. There were three different movements to fire me in the first five years. Suffice it to say, those days are rough to remember and impossible to forget. And this couple was one of the first to tell me, in no uncertain terms, *We're here, we're staying, and we're going to slog away with you.*

When I arrived at the church, the deacons were operating as de facto elders. Before long, some of them were restless to get rid of me. Hank, meanwhile, was quietly serving and building friendships within the church, including with some of these deacons. In fact, he so proved himself a servant and developed so much relational capital with the deacons that they decided to add him to their number. Somewhat ironically, then, Hank was the first true deacon, biblically defined, to join the board.

Once a deacon, he deftly navigated the swirling conflict. When it came to my leadership, he chose his battles but held his ground. Eventually Hank was made the chairman, partly because he was young (everyone else was nearing ninety) but also because he had won the deacons' trust. It still amazes me: for those patriarchs to have trusted Hank enough to make him chairman speaks volumes for the way he had handled things.

Sure enough, once the smoke cleared after those five years, what emerged was not only a different church but a different deacon board. Hank had never been to seminary or done vocational ministry, but he intuitively grasped how to do revitalization. So when the time came, in year six, to transition to elders, Hank was a key advocate given his clout as deacon chairman. He helped me immensely, steering the deacons' understanding of their biblical role in light of elder leadership. Our church's move to a plurality of elders would not have happened without the influence of this unlikely but exemplary deacon.[3]

———

Tim Ellis was the quintessential church member and model servant; respected by all, it seemed that he could do anything for anybody. Certainly it seemed like a no-brainer to install him as a deacon. There was just one sticking point: his wife was previously divorced. Even though most would say her divorce was biblical (her previous husband had committed adultery), nonetheless a cloud hovered over them both, as several older members were unwilling to consider him for the office given their take on "husband of one wife" (1 Tim. 3:12).

Several leaders were frustrated by this vocal minority, but Tim wasn't. In fact, his attitude was incredible. Essentially he said to us, *It's fine; I understand. Sometimes we need to meet people where they are. I'll just serve like a deacon anyway; you don't have to give me the title.* And this was not merely a nice sentiment; Tim served for years without any official title. When he was finally ordained as a deacon, it was a big win for the congregation, not to mention a prime teaching opportunity.

---

[3] Hank also coined a helpful shorthand to describe three broad categories of diaconal duties: (1) *building*: tending the grounds and dealing with repairs; (2) *bodies*: caring for people's physical needs; and (3) *borders*: taking responsibility for people's safety while they're on church property.

Two years later, Tim died in a car accident, leaving behind his wife and two young children. Tim was my neighbor and one of my closest friends; his death and subsequent absence remains one of the hardest things I've ever walked through. What kind of a legacy did this deacon leave? To this day, there is a phrase that floats around our church: the Tim Ellis Principle. In other words, *serve the Lord in whatever you do, regardless of whether anyone recognizes you.* Or to put it another way, live like Tim, the man who "deaconed" long before his church gave him the title.

———

I pastor an "underground" church in China, and on the Lord's Day we gather for worship in a rented hotel ballroom. For a while our home groups were assigned, on a rotating basis, to arrive early and stay late—setting up before the service and cleaning up after. Responsibilities also included preparing the elements for the Lord's Supper and welcoming new people.

Some complaints arose, however, for understandable reasons. First, not every member belongs to a home group, which meant some members were never assigned to serve. Second, it is not easy for families with young children to arrive early or leave late. (And besides, the kids would often make things messier while everyone else cleaned!) All of this led to some single members feeling frustrated because they ended up doing most of the work. I should also mention that we didn't have money to hire a cleaning person, nor would it have been wise to do so, for security reasons. Eventually it became clear: it was not feasible to continue this home-group rotation system.

So we decided to establish a deacon position to solve this problem. We installed a qualified brother into this "facility and hospitality" role and asked him to develop a plan to solve the problem. He soon presented his plan to our church's leaders, and we approved it.

The new system under diaconal leadership is a great improvement. All the members know their responsibilities and have been encouraged to love one another more and to better care for families with young kids. For the elders, it has been an excellent opportunity to teach the congregation about sacrifice, love, and faithfulness.

So often a deacon's job is to diminish conflict in the church. The best ones, I believe, do crucial work with no dramatic highlights. I am so grateful that God has used deacons in our church to help our people grow.

———

A few years ago, we had to ask an associate pastor to resign due to some prolonged relational disagreement and tension. Twenty or thirty members were hurt and confused; they loved this man and didn't understand why we couldn't just work it out. Because this group's trust in the elders was fractured, we felt unable to pastor them. We needed a mediator, someone to stand in the gap. One of our deacons, Jeff, rose to the occasion. He stepped into this delicate situation, which was fraught with tension, and he absorbed its shock. Amazingly, our relationship with the associate pastor was reconciled; he ended up staying at the church for another several months until he found a ministry opportunity elsewhere. And not a single person in the church left over this issue.

I'm convinced that none of this would have been possible without Jeff's wisdom and tenacity in pursuing peace. Most likely the associate pastor, along with many members, would have left. But because both the elders and the members trusted Deacon Jeff, he was the right mediator for the moment. And through it all, thanks to his initiative and servant leadership, our congregation was able to witness the beauty of biblical reconciliation.

———

Every time we celebrate the Lord's Supper, our deacon of ordinances arrives early to prepare the bread and arrange and fill the cups. He also gets there early to set up for baptisms and puts everything back in order after the service. He does all of this gladly.

This quiet labor makes possible something precious: the rest of us, pastors included, get to show up and participate in those two gospel reminders without any logistical hindrances. The fact that I get to focus on ministering through the ordinances and actually *enjoying* these events—without having to think about setup and takedown—enriches my experience as a pastor and our experience as a church family.

———

Here in Los Angeles, my husband and I run a small nonprofit that creates duffel bags for emergency foster-care placements. We also serve our church as deacons. Last year, a fellow deacon connected us with a lawyer who represents teenage girls in foster care who are also pregnant. At the time, this lawyer explained, there were three hundred pregnant girls in L.A.'s foster system. Sobered by this, the Lord gave us an idea: what if we could throw a baby shower for all of them?

Our church had recently inherited a beautiful building in the city, where our pastors were eager to let us host a shower. Thus began a remarkable collaborative effort between our small nonprofit and our church. The lawyer selected eleven girls in particularly vulnerable circumstances, each of whom we paired with a woman in our church. We so wanted this to feel like a baby shower, not merely a foster event. We prayed that these girls would feel the same level of love and anticipation that many of us did at our own showers. Though I coordinated this effort, our whole church rose to the occasion, donating an amazing $3,000 worth of items.

The shower had all the works: flowers, fancy food, a coffee cart, table games, a photo booth, and more—all donated and organized by sisters in the church. At the time, our nonprofit had an unbelieving intern who'd never set foot inside a church building; she was startled and amazed to see, for the first time, Christian love. On the day of the shower, the girls were each given a crib, high chair, embroidered bag, formula, diapers, stuffed animals, and a year's worth of baby clothes. A photographer came and took professional portraits of each girl, which were stunning and dignifying. Our goal was modest: we simply wanted to find ways to honor these girls in their decision to choose life in the face of dire challenges, to celebrate them for having little and yet still walking into this brave choice. What a privilege to be able to offer a small glimpse of God's heart for the downtrodden. Our work as deacons simply spearheaded an effort that allowed so many to serve together. I will never forget it.

———

We were a young church plant in Australia. We did not own a building and were renting space for weekly worship. Tim was our deacon who coordinated Sunday logistics; in fact, he served in the role even before we began to officially recognize deacons in the church.

I don't recall Tim doing anything from the front, but behind the scenes he made a profound difference. He organized all of the church's volunteer rosters—from children's ministry to sound team to music team to welcoming team to setup to takedown. Week after week, we entered a room that had been fully prepared for the worship of God and edification of his people thanks to this brother's humble service.

Tim didn't serve in ways that grabbed the attention of the world; in many cases he served in ways that wouldn't be seen by anyone except Jesus. His labor enabled the elders to concentrate on the ministry of the Word and prayer. And I'm sure it saved the church from all sorts of complications and potential conflicts. We were immensely grateful for Tim's service week in and week out during that season.

———

Last year a man in our church—in his forties, with a wife and three kids—experienced a debilitating neurological problem. He was able to return home from the hospital after being near death, yet it was unclear whether he would ever walk again—and then only with the aid of a walker. In the meantime, a wheelchair was going to be a new part of his life—but his house wasn't wheelchair accessible. Our deacons sprang into action! In less than a week they managed to design and build a ramp into the house, and they laid new flooring in a main-level room that would serve as a bedroom. It was truly remarkable to see.

An additional story occurred during the COVID-19 shutdown, as we learned of "food deserts" around our city—pockets of lower-income residents with little access to food due to loss of income. So our deacons organized a food drive; for two days, they put on gloves and masks and received deliveries of canned goods and dried foods from our church members. We were able to collect two truckloads of food! The deacons delivered it all to a drop-off hub, where local churches within the immediate food-desert area would then distribute it to those in need.

———

I pastor a small, rural church in East Texas. About a year ago, James—an elderly man with meager means and poor health—completed the membership process and gladly became part of our church family. As a younger man, James had served in the American military and also pastored a few small churches; now he is a widower and a rather secluded retiree. It didn't take me long to realize that this man had many practical needs and that I simply couldn't care well for him by myself.

David is a jolly and kindhearted deacon, always looking for ways to serve others, and he was glad to connect with James. David drives about thirty minutes out of his way to pick up James for men's Bible study each Friday morning. Regularly, David taxis James into town to visit the grocery store and run a few errands. James was recently admitted to the hospital due to some lung complications—David was the first to know and the first to reassure him in the midst of that stressful time.

David has taken on many simple yet time-consuming tasks in the life of our church's ministry, and he has met countless practical needs among our church's membership. One major reason I am able to devote adequate time to the ministry of the Word and prayer is because of David's eager and loving service. I praise God for him.

THE COMMON DENOMINATOR

Can you see the tremendous impact of effective deacons? They assist their pastors and enrich the life of the church in manifold ways: organizing service, tackling tangible needs, shielding the ministry of the Word, guarding the harmony of the flock, caring for the distressed, and so much more.

No doubt locations and circumstances vary greatly, but the common denominator—the heartbeat—of diaconal work remains the same: self-giving service for the good of Christ's church and the glory of his name.

6

THE BEAUTY:
WHO DEACONS REFLECT

Isaac is discouraged. It's been twelve years since he was installed as a deacon at Riverside Church, and some days he wonders why he ever agreed to it. *I've poured so much into this church, and no one ever notices or cares,* Isaac thinks. *I'm not looking for effusive praise, but a "thank you" every now and then would be nice.*

Isaac coordinates the church's ministry to homebound members, those whose health prevents them from making it on Sundays. He's spent untold hours in the homes of Riverside's senior saints, replacing lightbulbs and installing handrails and building ramps. Isaac doesn't begrudge manual labor, and he does have a knack for it, but it irks him when church members quip that his "love language" must be acts of service. (He doesn't recall having a choice.)

One of my aims in this book has been to recover some of the dignity, and even the glory, of diaconal service. But is that just a nice sentiment, easy to advocate on paper but a pipe dream amid the real stuff of life? After all, deacons like Isaac in churches like Riverside are likely more typical than we imagine. Many deacons *are* running low on energy and encouragement, drained of motivation and joy. Maybe that describes a deacon in your church. Maybe it describes you.

As we approach the finish line of this book, I want to reiterate that diaconal work is not glorious because it is always seen (it often isn't). Nor is it glorious because it always gratifies (it often doesn't). Ultimately, the work is glorious because of what it mirrors.

ISAIAH'S FORECAST

When Jesus walked the earth, the office of deacon did not exist. And yet his life had everything to do with it. To grasp the significance of Jesus's impact on deaconing, though, we must rewind the story to see how the Old Testament fills the diaconal narrative with meaning.

The theme of Israel as God's chosen servant gains particular prominence in the book of Isaiah, written seven hundred years prior to Jesus's arrival on earth:

> But you, Israel, my servant,
>   Jacob, whom I have chosen,
>   the offspring of Abraham, my friend;
> you whom I took from the ends of the earth,
>   and called from its farthest corners,
> saying to you, "You are my servant,
>   I have chosen you and not cast you off." (Isa. 41:8–9;
>   cf. 43:10; 44:1–2)

However, even the nation's high status as God's chosen servant was insufficient to rescue them from the penalty of their sin. Nevertheless God, ever rich in mercy, promised pardon:

Remember these things, O Jacob,
and Israel, for you are my servant;
I formed you; you are my servant;
O Israel, you will not be forgotten by me.
I have blotted out your transgressions like a cloud
and your sins like mist;
return to me, for I have redeemed you. (Isa. 44:21–22;
cf. 48:20)

Moreover, this blessing of forgiveness was never meant for Israel alone. God's aim, ever since Abram's call (Gen. 12:3), was for his servant people to mediate his blessing to the world:

[The LORD] says:
"It is too light a thing that you should be my servant
to raise up the tribes of Jacob
and to bring back the preserved of Israel;
I will make you as a light for the nations,
that my salvation may reach to the end of the earth." (Isa. 49:6)

And yet for all of this "national" attention, Isaiah's camera also zooms in on a sole individual, one who would represent the entire nation. Let's back up to hear how the first "servant song" begins:

Behold my servant, whom I uphold,
my chosen, in whom my soul delights;
I have put my Spirit upon him;
he will bring forth justice to the nations. (Isa. 42:1)

By the time we reach Isaiah's final servant song, the camera lens has settled into place: the emblematic servant is in full view. It is one of the most prophetically pregnant passages in all the Hebrew Scriptures. In just fifteen verses, from Isaiah 52:13 to 53:12, God makes clear that his servant's exaltation will not come apart from the humiliation of sin-bearing death:

> Behold, my servant shall act wisely;
>> he shall be high and lifted up,
>> and shall be exalted. . . .
>
> Yet it was the will of the LORD to crush him;
>> he has put him to grief;
> when his soul makes an offering for guilt,
>> he shall see his offspring; he shall prolong his days;
> the will of the LORD shall prosper in his hand.
> Out of the anguish of his soul he shall see and be satisfied;
> by his knowledge shall the righteous one, my servant,
>> make many to be accounted righteous,
>> and he shall bear their iniquities. (Isa. 52:13; 53:10–11)

And what results from the suffering servant's death and resurrection? Gentiles stream into the family as servants of the living God:

> And the foreigners who join themselves to the LORD,
>> to minister to him, to love the name of the LORD,
>> and to be his servants,
> everyone who keeps the Sabbath and does not profane it,
>> and holds fast my covenant—
> these I will bring to my holy mountain,
>> and make them joyful in my house of prayer;
> their burnt offerings and their sacrifices
>> will be accepted on my altar;

for my house shall be called a house of prayer
for *all* peoples. (Isa. 56:6–7)

Zooming out, an aerial shot of Isaiah's entire scroll reveals something astonishing: the king (chapters 1–37) is the servant (38–55) is the conqueror (56–66). He is the same person. And zooming out even farther, a new link in the Bible's unfolding story clicks into place: God's suffering servant is none other than God's holy king (2 Sam. 7:12–13) through whom God's blessing spreads (Gen. 12:3) and God's enemy dies (Gen. 3:15).

KING OF KINGS, DEACON OF DEACONS

So when Jesus finally arrives on the scene, he is not appearing in a vacuum. Dozens of promises and centuries of pent-up longing—"the hopes and fears of all the years," as the familiar carol puts it—are curiously taking shape around one Galilean day laborer from an obscure backwater town in the mightiest empire on earth. And when he launches his public ministry, he wastes no time identifying himself as the subject of Isaiah's ancient song. For all the melodies were about him:

> And he came to Nazareth, where he had been brought up. And as was his custom, he went to the synagogue on the Sabbath day, and he stood up to read. And the scroll of the prophet Isaiah was given to him. He unrolled the scroll and found the place where it was written,
>
> > "The Spirit of the Lord is upon me,
> > because he has anointed me

> to proclaim good news to the poor.
> He has sent me to proclaim liberty to the captives
>   and recovering of sight to the blind,
>   to set at liberty those who are oppressed,
> to proclaim the year of the Lord's favor."

> And he rolled up the scroll and gave it back to the attendant
> and sat down. And the eyes of all in the synagogue were fixed
> on him. And he began to say to them, "Today this Scripture has
> been fulfilled in your hearing." (Luke 4:16–21)

Jesus has come to embody the scope of Israel's purpose, to succeed where the nation failed and ultimately to be exiled on a pagan cross. In the meantime, he will teach his followers the astonishing secret to true greatness and the downward mobility of real kingdom life:

> Jesus called them to him and said to them, "You know that
> those who are considered rulers of the Gentiles lord it over
> them, and their great ones exercise authority over them. But it
> shall not be so among you. But whoever would be great among
> you must be your servant [*diakonos*], and whoever would be
> first among you must be slave of all. For even the Son of Man
> came not to be served [*diakonēthēnai*] but to serve [*diakonēsai*],
> and to give his life as a ransom for many." (Mark 10:42–45;
> cf. 9:34–35)

The world has always measured greatness by the standard of service a person *receives*, not by what he gives. But Jesus radically reverses our fallen logic. "He [does] not make subtle changes or adjustments in a well-entrenched system," one theologian observes. "He [turns] the whole thing upside down, making . . . the first last and the last first."[1] And how does he do this? How does he inaugurate standards that subvert the way of the world? "He does it by demonstration. He 'deacons.' Place high value on that word; it rises from the heart of the gospel."[2]

In anticipation of his final meal with his disciples, Jesus makes arrangements to have the room and the supper prepared. Stepping through the door that afternoon, the disciples are not surprised by the smell of food wafting from the table. Nor are they surprised to see a towel and water basin on the floor. There is only one glaring omission. *Where is the servant?* The last thing in the world they expect is to watch their great master kneel down, assuming the posture and role of a nobody—a slave!—in order to cleanse their filthy feet. But he does. Then, like clockwork, seemingly before their feet have fully dried, a spat erupts over which disciple is the greatest. Jesus interrupts the pathetic quarrel: "For who is greater, the one at the table or the one serving [*diakonōn*]? Isn't it the one at the table? But I am among you as the one who serves [*diakonōn*]" (Luke 22:27 CSB).

Tim Keller draws two implications for diaconal work from this story. His words are hard-hitting:

> First of all, Jesus washed feet despite his impending death. Jesus was to have the wrath of God poured out on him. He was feeling the tremendous weight of that even at the supper. When we are hurting, with a load of care on our backs, do we

---

[1] George C. Fuller, "The High Calling of Deacon," in Timothy J. Keller, *Resources for Deacons: Love Expressed through Mercy Ministries* (Lawrenceville, GA: Presbyterian Church in America Committee on Discipleship Ministries, 1985), 7.

[2] Fuller, "High Calling of Deacon," 7.

look around and notice that people's feet need to be washed? Do we look for little ways to serve? No! We are usually absorbed in our troubles, and we want people to take care of us. . . . A real servant does not say, "When I get my life together, when I get over my blues, when I get my schedule in order, then I will start to minister." Perhaps you are hurting, and you may even be angry because no one is noticing. But where would you be if Jesus had your attitude?

Second, Jesus served despite the unworthiness of the disciples. Notice John's reminder that Jesus knew the betrayer was present (13:2, 10). Jesus saw them all—one betrayer, one denier, all forsakers! When he needed them most, they would leave him. One of those sets of feet was dirty and sore from an errand that arranged for his torture and death. What did Jesus do? He washed those feet.[3]

In ancient Greek society this sort of behavior was not inspiring; it was absurd. It was not beautiful; it was repugnant. "How," Plato had asked four centuries earlier, "can a man be happy who is the servant of anything?"[4] And yet here is God's eternal Son, on the floor, dignifying the most menial labor in the world.

CHRIST'S ONGOING DIACONAL MINISTRY

Jesus's earthly ministry was mighty in both word and deed (cf. Luke 24:19), and he continues this two-pronged approach today in large part through the offices of elder and deacon. As elders serve with words and deacons serve with deeds, Christ's

[3] Timothy J. Keller, *Ministries of Mercy: The Call of the Jericho Road*, 2nd ed. (Phillipsburg, NJ: P&R, 1997), 138.
[4] Plato, *Dialogues of Plato: Translated into English, with Analyses and Introduction*, vol. 3, trans. Benjamin Jowett (Cambridge: Cambridge University Press, 2010), 86.

holistic ministry carries on. "Christ cares for his church through the officers he chooses," observe William Boekestein and Daniel Hyde. And deacons, they contend, are a means by which he continues part of his priestly work.[5] As Ignatius of Antioch—who may have been born as early as AD 35—simply asserts, deacons have been "entrusted with the service of Jesus Christ."[6]

By caring for the hurting, deacons function as Christ's hands and feet to a world that needs his touch. As they discern and meet practical needs, deacons reflect the Savior who took the ultimate initiative to meet our deepest need. And by acting as "shock absorbers," who both protect and promote church unity, deacons please the One who both prayed for it (John 17:21–22) and bled to secure it (Eph. 2:11–22).

No wonder Paul can summarize the incarnation by simply stating that "Christ became a servant [*diakonos*]" (Rom. 15:8). Elsewhere he elaborates, in one of Scripture's most breathtaking passages:

> Do nothing from selfish ambition or conceit, but in humility count others more significant than yourselves. Let each of you look not only to his own interests, but also to the interests of others. Have this mind among yourselves, which is yours in Christ Jesus, who, though he was in the form of God, did not count equality with God a thing to be grasped, but

---

[5] William Boekestein and Daniel R. Hyde, *A Well-Ordered Church: Laying a Foundation for a Vibrant Church* (Darlington, UK: Evangelical Press, 2015), 49, 45, original emphasis removed. On similarities between the Old Testament office of priest and the New Testament office of deacon, see Daniel R. Hyde, "Rulers and Servants: The Nature of and Qualifications for the Offices of Elder and Deacon," in *Called to Serve: Essays for Elders and Deacons*, ed. Michael Brown (Middleville, MI: Reformed Fellowship, 2006), 6–10.
[6] Ignatius of Antioch, *Epistle to the Magnesians* 6.1.

emptied himself, by taking the form of a servant, being born in the likeness of men. And being found in human form, he humbled himself by becoming obedient to the point of death, even death on a cross. Therefore God has highly exalted him and bestowed on him the name that is above every name, so that at the name of Jesus every knee should bow, in heaven and on earth and under the earth, and every tongue confess that Jesus Christ is Lord, to the glory of God the Father. (Phil. 2:3–11)

Various religions in history have acknowledged the value of humility; none has dared speak of a humble God. The notion of humility applied to deity is simply seen as category confusion. So the claim that the God of the Bible—not a member of a pantheon, not an option on a menu of deities, but the one Creator of all—that *he* would stoop to serve his creatures, all the way down to a torturous cross, is not just startling; it's scandalous.

But that's precisely what happened. Philippians 2 resounds with the news that even though God the Son had it *all*—the worship of angels, the infinite love of Father and Spirit—he still came. From the splendor of heaven to the squalor of a stable. And on a lonely night in a little town called Bethlehem, he began a journey of obedience to his Father— a journey that would culminate thirty-three years later on a hill outside Jerusalem, where he suffered on a Roman cross for rebels like us. And what compelled him? *Indescribable love*. Indeed, "greater love has no one than this, that someone lay down his life for his friends" (John 15:13). There is no more perfect example of self-giving service than the One who left heaven when he could have stayed, and who stayed on the cross when he could have left.

So, deacon, lift your eyes from the mundane to the Messiah. See him touching unclean hands and washing filthy feet and serving ungrateful sinners and finally relinquishing his life for those he loves. The entire shape of diaconal service finds its model and its mission in the life of your Savior.

Deacon, your office has an expiration date, but your status as the King's servant will never end. Why would it? Life in his service is perfect freedom. Your current role as a deacon is just an internship for an eternal future in which you will see his face, together with all his servants, world without end:

> No longer will there be anything accursed, but the throne of God and of the Lamb will be in it, and his servants will worship him. (Rev. 22:3; cf. v. 6)

May Jesus, the ultimate *diakonos*, return in glory soon. Isaiah's songs have been fulfilled, but there is an encore coming.

CONCLUSION

Deacons Are Difference-Makers

Modern Western culture is, in many respects, an experiment in virtue inversion. Former virtues are increasingly seen as vices, and former vices as virtues. Of course, some changes have done enormous good, as historically oppressed and disadvantaged groups—women and African Americans, for example—have been granted rights long overdue. Praise God.

But not every cultural shift has been positive. Take, for instance, self-denial. In many traditional cultures this was generally a virtue: you subdue your own desires for the larger good of your family or nation or class (those "beneath" you, as we saw with Plato, are a different story). Yet now in the West the idea of suppressing your own desires for *anyone*—even family or peers—is often viewed as naïve or unenlightened, even cultural heresy. "You do you" no longer points to selfishness, but to wellness. It is not easy, it turns out, to deny yourself and be true to yourself at the same time.

What does this mini-analysis of our cultural moment have to do with deacons? Everything—since their work is, at its core, self-giving service for the good of another. As the world shouts "Assert yourself," godly deacons look for ways to deny themselves. As the world beckons "Serve yourself," deacons are busy strategizing ways to serve others. And as the pervasive world of social media urges "Promote yourself," deacons quietly set others up to win. It's not that traditional cultures were morally pristine until expressive individualism showed up and ruined everything. Yet no culture in history has done more than ours to broadcast mantras and implant a mindset that runs so contrary to the heart of diaconal work.

Self-denying service has always been challenging. Has it ever been so countercultural?

SERVANT SETH

In chapter 1, we met several stereotypical deacons—Pastor-in-Training Peter, Toolbox Terrance, Spreadsheet Sam, Corporate Cliff, Veto Vinnie, and Pseudo-Elder Steve.

It's time to meet one more.

You've already met him, it turns out, because Servant Seth is who we've been talking about for much of this book. He isn't gunning for an office, a title, or a spotlight. In fact, he knows that doing deeds "to be seen by others" is what marks *opponents* of his Savior (Matt. 23:5). Seth has internalized the upside-down nature of true greatness, described by Jesus himself:

> The greatest among you shall be your servant [*diakonos*]. Whoever exalts himself will be humbled, and whoever humbles himself will be exalted. (Matt. 23:11–12)

In short, Seth gets it: as one ministry leader observed, a deacon who is above the people is below the office.[1]

Don't misunderstand. Seth is not perfect, but he is prayerful and growing in humility. He's not the smartest guy in the room, but he is teachable. He's not the most experienced guy in the room, but he is respected because of the way he treats people. Seth is not a "yes man," but he's also not a self-appointed pastoral critic. He doesn't think it's his job—or any Christian's, for that matter—to gaze suspiciously at godly leaders. Seth loves to fade into the background, not because he's falsely modest but because he cares about what's foregrounded in the church: the glory of Jesus Christ. And he knows that the brightness of Christ's glory will be eclipsed if the pastors are perpetually distracted by administrative problems. Seth enjoys facilitating ministry and handling logistics so the elders can concentrate their energies on leading and shepherding the congregation through the ministry of the Word and prayer. And, what's more, he is motivated by love! He embodies the words of Paul: "For Christ's love compels us, . . . that those who live should no longer live for themselves but for him who died for them and was raised again" (2 Cor. 5:14–15 NIV).

Wouldn't Seth make an ideal deacon? Yes, because he's a growing, mature believer. Is he known among the church for his character, his humility, his eagerness to creatively and quietly serve? Check, check, check.

---

[1] Tony Wolfe, personal correspondence, April 2, 2020. Tony is the director of pastor/church relations for the Southern Baptists of Texas Convention (SBCTX) and the author of *A Deacon on Purpose: Four Biblical Essentials*, a book and video curriculum produced by SBCTX in 2018.

DEACONS WERE HERE

Faithful deacons should be able to see their fingerprints on every sermon that's preached. *Our pastor would not be able to do that, or not nearly so effectively, if I were not doing this.*

Faithful deacons should see their fingerprints in the unity of their congregation, for which Jesus prayed (John 17:22). *Today there are brothers and sisters in this church living together in love and harmony, who otherwise wouldn't be.*

Indeed, faithful deacons should see their fingerprints in the welfare of all the flock and in the church's worldwide witness. *Because I saw that need and rose to meet it, the elders were freed to focus on shepherding eternal souls. Because I recruited those volunteers, our pastor didn't have to spend his Saturday doing it. Because I deferred to the elders' collective wisdom on that complex issue, a younger deacon learned the value of humble respect. Because I loved that senior saint in her distress, she was lifted from her despair and made more eager to see Christ's face. Because I quelled that conflict, the gospel was able to go forth in power.*

I don't know why you picked up this book, but I do know this: deacons were God's idea. He loves deacons, and he wants us to also. But in order to rightly love the office we must understand the Bible's glorious vision for it. No, we shouldn't elevate deacons to an executive board of pseudo-elders. It is an office of service, not oversight. But let us not reduce the role to savvy businessmen or skilled handymen either. Deacons are so much more. They are an influential cavalry of servants, called by the King and deputized by his church to target and meet tangible needs. To protect and promote church unity. To enhance the ministry of the elders. And, in doing so, to accelerate the mission of the church.

Deacons do physical work with spiritual effect, and invisible work with palpable effect. Their calling is noble. Their service is needed. And their reward is near (1 Tim. 3:13).

Appendix 1

MAY WOMEN SERVE AS DEACONS?

If you flipped here before reading the rest of the book, shame on you. Return to the Table of Contents and try again.

I'm kidding, of course. That this question arrests our attention isn't just understandable; it's unavoidable. Every single church with deacons must, in one way or another, come to a conclusion on whether Christ calls women to the office. Sometimes that decision is formal, codified in a church constitution or denominational document; other times it's less formal, driven largely by custom. Either way, the choice must be made: will the office of deacon in your church be open to women or not?

My aim in this appendix is to offer what I believe are the strongest arguments for both views, leaving you to decide which is most compelling. (Full disclosure: my own view is that it *is* biblical to have women deacons. Note my comments in the concluding two paragraphs of this appendix.)

ARGUMENTS AGAINST WOMEN DEACONS

Sometimes, those convinced that Scripture limits the diaconate to qualified men are accused of not valuing the ministry of women. But this conclusion doesn't necessarily follow from the premise. Women can absolutely flourish in churches without women deacons. Their worth can be valued, their gifts celebrated, their contributions encouraged, their ministry championed.

Now, surely some churches restrict the office to men out of a low view of the ministry of women. *Stay out of the way and leave real ministry to us!* But the existence of "ministerial chauvinism" in some male-deacon-only churches doesn't mean it infects every such church. Yes, one church may have pathetic reasons for limiting the office to men, but what if another church's reasons are different? What if their reasons are carefully thought out? No doubt plenty of churches *without* women deacons encourage and equip women better than other churches who technically have them but who, when it comes to the "real work" of theology and ministry, continue to keep women at arm's length.

That said, here is a case for limiting the diaconal office to qualified men.

1. The Jerusalem Church Selected Only Men

As we saw in chapter 2, Luke is clear about the qualifications for the seven who were appointed to serve the Jerusalem church:

> And the twelve summoned the full number of the disciples and said, "It is not right that we should give up preaching the word of God to serve tables. Therefore, brothers, pick out from among you seven men of good repute, full of the Spirit and of wisdom, whom we will appoint to this duty." (Acts 6:2–3)

Not "seven women," not "a few of each." Seven *men*.

Now, it's true that Acts 6 doesn't technically feature the office of deacon, but surely the passage sets in motion a pattern that soon becomes the position (cf. Phil. 1:1). And besides, it isn't as if we hesitate to draw deacon-related principles from the story. I proposed several in chapter 2: "word ministry" is prioritized, the congregation is involved, character is foregrounded, labor is divided, the seven solve a problem and thereby safeguard church unity, and so on.

It seems arbitrary, then, to omit from our applications this one principle: that deacons today, like the seven who preceded them, should be exclusively male.

2. Paul Referred to Deacons' Wives, Not Women Deacons

In his list of deacon qualifications, Paul includes four qualifications for their wives:

> Deacons likewise must be dignified, not double-tongued, not addicted to much wine, not greedy for dishonest gain. They must hold the mystery of the faith with a clear conscience. And let them also be tested first; then let them serve as deacons if they prove themselves blameless. Their wives [*gynaikas*] likewise must be dignified, not slanderers, but sober-minded, faithful in all things. Let deacons each be the husband of one wife, managing their children and their own households well. For those who serve well as deacons gain a good standing for themselves and also great confidence in the faith that is in Christ Jesus. (1 Tim. 3:8–13)

It's true that the Greek word at the outset of verse 11, rendered here as "wives" (*gynaikas*), can also be translated "women." But

137

in the flow of this section a reference to deacons' wives is more likely, for several reasons.

First, in the immediate context of chapter 3, the word is twice translated "wife," not "woman" (vv. 2, 12). Thus, the natural way to read the chapter's only other occurrence, in verse 11, is also as "wives."

Second, if Paul is referring to women *deacons*, then why doesn't he assign them that title, as he's previously done for both elders (v. 1) and deacons (v. 8)? Why use an ambiguous word (*gynaikas*, "wives" or "women") rather than a more specific designation like *diakonous* with the feminine article—whether *tas diakonous* ("female deacons") or *gynaikas diakonous* ("women deacons")?

Third, Paul stipulates marriage standards for both elders (v. 2) and male deacons (v. 12); why not for these women if they are deacons, too? He also omits any testing requirement, unlike for the elders (v. 6; cf. 5:22) and deacons (v. 10).

Fourth, it's difficult to imagine why Paul would discuss male deacons (vv. 8–10), then female deacons (v. 11), then male deacons again (v. 12). If he were truly turning his attention from male deacons to female deacons, why suddenly return to male deacons in the next verse? It is better to conclude that Paul is speaking of male deacons throughout, and is here examining one's family life from two angles: the character of his wife (v. 11) and his own character as both husband and father (v. 12).

Lastly, given the nature of diaconal responsibility, it makes sense that Paul would include some qualifications for their wives. As Guy Waters explains, "In light of the sensitivities surrounding deacons' work, and in light of the fact that wives may be called on to assist their husbands—particularly in addressing the needs of the church's women—one could see why Paul might have desired that the church be satisfied with the character of a candidate *and* his wife as they assessed his suitability for the diaconate."[1]

3. Phoebe Was a Servant, Not a Deacon

In Romans 16, Paul's personal greetings begin with a commendation of Phoebe:

> I commend to you our sister Phoebe, a servant [*diakonos*] of the church at Cenchreae, that you may welcome her in the Lord in a way worthy of the saints, and help her in whatever she may need from you, for she has been a patron of many and of myself as well. (Rom. 16:1–2)

Though the word here is indeed *diakonos*, we know from the rest of the New Testament that the word is almost always used informally, in reference to a person we might today describe as "ministry-minded" or "servant-hearted." This is no exception. And if the usage here has a technical meaning at all, it is more likely "courier" or "envoy" rather than "deacon."[2] That is, Phoebe may have been a designated letter-carrier on behalf of the Cenchrean church, a far cry from the formal office of deacon. Moreover, it is misguided to draw any significance

---

[1] Guy Waters, "Does the Bible Support Female Deacons? No" (The Gospel Coalition. Article available at www.tgc.org/article/bible-support-female-deacons-no [emphasis original]).

[2] Clarence D. Agan III, "Deacons, Deaconesses, and Denominational Discussions: Romans 16:1 as a Test Case," *Presbyterion: Covenant Seminary Review* 34/2 (Fall 2008): 105–08.

from the word's masculine ending, since the feminine form (*diakonissa*) hadn't yet been coined.

In sum, nothing in the context of Romans 16 demands that we view Phoebe as anything more than a dedicated and praiseworthy servant sent, perhaps on some official business, by the Cenchrean church.

4. Diaconal Work Entails a Measure of Authority

The qualifications for deacons in 1 Timothy 3 follow closely on the heels of a gender-specific prohibition:

> Let a woman learn quietly with all submissiveness. I do not permit a woman to teach or to exercise authority over a man; rather, she is to remain quiet. For Adam was formed first, then Eve; and Adam was not deceived, but the woman was deceived and became a transgressor. Yet she will be saved through child-bearing—if they continue in faith and love and holiness, with self-control. (1 Tim. 2:11–15)

Though believers will doubtless debate applications, from a complementarian perspective this much is clear: women may not exercise formal spiritual authority over men in the church, and therefore may not serve as elders. As the rest of the letter makes clear, elders are distinguished from deacons by their unique calling to both teach and govern the whole church (3:2; 5:17), tasks which correspond precisely to these two female-specific prohibitions: "teach" and "exercise authority" (2:12).

In sum, the *prohibitions* (1 Tim. 2:12) should inform our reading of the *qualifications* (3:11) such that, however we apply the latter passage, we do not practically undermine the former.

But avoiding this is difficult, if not impossible, since real influence and leadership and, yes, some measure of authority will naturally accrue to a skilled deacon. It is perhaps noteworthy, too, that a deacon must "manage" (*proistamenoi*) his household well (v. 12). Might this suggest that, as with elders (vv. 4–5), the diaconate involves functions that should be echoes of one's leadership at home? To open the diaconate to women is therefore not just unbiblical but also unwise, for they will inevitably take on a level of practical authority that Scripture forbids.[3]

ARGUMENTS FOR WOMEN DEACONS

Turning now to arguments *for* installing women in diaconal positions, an important caveat is in order: this case assumes that the deacons in your church operate like deacons, not elders. If your deacons basically function as a governing elder board, then it seems best to continue limiting the diaconal office to men for now. Your first assignment is to study and implement what God's Word says not about *women* deacons but about deacons in general. (And if you've made it this far in the book and have no clue about that topic, then I've failed spectacularly!)

Now, disclaimer aside, here are some arguments for opening the diaconate to qualified women.

1. Scripture Nowhere Forbids Women Deacons

We've already seen Paul's prohibition regarding the office and function of elder: "I do not permit a woman to teach or to

---

[3] As official representatives or agents of the elders, Alexander Strauch contends, deacons "hold authority and a place of leadership over men and women within the congregation" (Alexander Strauch, "Does the Bible Allow for Women Deacons? No, Says Alex Strauch [with a Response from Tom Schreiner]," *9Marks Journal*, December 2019).

exercise authority over a man" (1 Tim. 2:12). Elders uniquely are charged with teaching and giving spiritual oversight to the whole church. To be sure, deacons will need to make decisions about resources, call upon others for help, and generally manage areas of tangible need, as the seven's management of the food distribution surely implies (Acts 6:1–7).

But unlike elders, deacons are not charged with shepherding the whole flock (Acts 20:28; 1 Pet. 5:2). Unlike elders, deacons need not stand ready to "give instruction in sound doctrine and . . . rebuke those who contradict it" (Titus 1:9). Unlike elders, deacons will not answer to God for the spiritual welfare of individual souls (Heb. 13:17). Never once do we read a verse like "Be subject to the deacons" (cf. 1 Pet. 5:5), or "Obey your deacons and submit to them" (cf. Heb. 13:17), for such language is exclusively applied to the office of elder.

In short, there is no "1 Timothy 2:12 equivalent" for deacons, since theirs is not an office of spiritual authority and is therefore naturally open to qualified women. Why forbid what the Bible doesn't?

2. Paul Referred to Women Deacons, Not Deacons' Wives

Back to the qualifications in 1 Timothy 3:

> Deacons likewise must be dignified, not double-tongued, not addicted to much wine, not greedy for dishonest gain. They must hold the mystery of the faith with a clear conscience. And let them also be tested first; then let them serve as deacons if they prove themselves blameless. Their wives [*gynaikas*] likewise must be dignified, not slanderers, but sober-minded,

faithful in all things. Let deacons each be the husband of one
wife, managing their children and their own households well.
For those who serve well as deacons gain a good standing for
themselves and also great confidence in the faith that is in
Christ Jesus. (1 Tim. 3:8–13)

Again, *gynaikas* (v. 11) can mean either "wives" or "women"
(e.g., ESV "their wives"; NIV "the women"; NASB "women"),
the proper translation depending on context. And verse 11 is
best translated "women"—as in women deacons—for several
reasons.

First, Paul uses *gynaikas* eight other times in 1 Timothy—
arguably all of which are best translated "women," not "wives."
The first five examples (2:9, 10, 11, 12, 14) are undisputed.
But what about the two in the immediate context of 3:11?

- 3:2: "husband of one wife" (*mias gynaikos andra*)
- 3:12: "husband[s] of one wife" (*mias gynaikos andres*)

On first glance, this translation ("wife") may seem the only rea-
sonable option. But, literally rendered, the phrase is just "one-
woman man" (3:2) and "one-woman men" (3:12). Nothing
about this qualification *demands* the translation "wife"; in fact,
the slightly broader focus of "woman" helpfully encompasses
more diaconal candidates, such as single men and widowers. The
point is that the man's fidelity—in relationships with women
other than his wife—is broadly known and uncontroversial.[4]

---

[4] Thabiti Anyabwile offers several helpful questions and observations for assessing both
single and married candidates. See his chapter 10, "A One-Woman Man," in *Finding
Faithful Elders and Deacons* (Wheaton, IL: Crossway, 2012), 61–65.

On this point it is also worth observing that, out of Paul's nine uses of *gynaikas* in 1 Timothy, only one bears the exact same structure as 3:11:

- "Likewise also . . . women . . ." (2:9)
- "Women likewise . . ." (3:11 NASB, ESV mg, cf. NIV)

And since the first (2:9) is clearly referencing women, not wives, we should default to hearing its later echo (3:11) in the same way.

Second, the possessive pronoun "their"—as in "their wives" (v. 11)—is not in the text. It is sometimes inserted to support the translation "wives," but it is not originally present. Paul could easily have included a qualifier—say, "their" (*autōn*) or "their own" (*idiōn*)—to clearly specify a focus on deacon wives, but he did not.[5] This hints that his bare use of *gynaikas*, without the pronoun, means he has women deacons in view.

Third, consider the paragraph's grammatical structure:

- v. 8: "Deacons likewise must be dignified . . ." (followed by three qualifications)
- v. 11: "Wives/women likewise must be dignified . . ." (followed by three qualifications)

These verses stand in exact parallel, each featuring the word "likewise," followed by "dignified," followed by three addi-

---

[5] "If *the wives of the deacons* or of the clergy were meant . . . it would be natural to have it unambiguously expressed, e.g., by the addition of [*autōn*]." The possessive is not implied and one is not supplied. (Quote from Newport J. D. White, *The First and Second Epistles to Timothy and the Epistle to Titus*, in *The Expositor's Greek Testament*, vol. 4 [1897; repr., Grand Rapids, MI: Eerdmans, 1956], 116. See also Jennifer H. Stiefel, "Women Deacons in 1 Timothy: A Linguistic and Literary Look at 'Women Likewise . . .' (1 Tim. 3:11)," *New Testament Studies* 41/3 [July 1995]: 442–57).

tional qualifications. This use of "likewise" (NIV "in the same way"), echoing verse 8, suggests that Paul is still discussing deacons. The women serve just as the men do.

Fourth, even more significant is how these verses function identically—and therefore together—in relation to an earlier one:

- v. 2: "An overseer must be . . ."
- v. 8: "Deacons likewise [must be] . . ."
- v. 11: "Wives/women likewise [must be] . . ."

This "zoomed out" view of the whole passage suggests that the women in verse 11 are not fundamentally distinguished *from the deacons*, but *from the elders*. Paul is treating the women and the deacons together, as one office, in parallel relation to the elders, the other office.

Fifth, what about the common objection that seeing women deacons in verse 11 amounts to linguistic whiplash? It's a good question: why *would* Paul discuss deacons (vv. 8–10), then jump to women deacons (v. 11), then go right back to (clearly male) deacons (v. 12)? I'm dizzy just writing it!

The answer is actually quite simple: Paul "bookends" the paragraph with general statements pertaining to all deacons (vv. 8–10 and v. 13), inside of which he addresses, with brief specificity, both female (v. 11) and male (v. 12) deacons. Tracing these structural clues helps crystallize the flow of thought:

- qualifications for elders (vv. 1–7)
- general qualifications for deacons (vv. 8–10)

- specific qualifications for female deacons (v. 11)[6]
- specific qualifications for male deacons (v. 12)
- summary for all deacons (v. 13)

Sixth, the character traits demanded of these women are also required for both elders and male deacons—which makes sense if an official capacity is intended. The women must be "sober-minded" just as elders are (v. 2) and "dignified" just as deacons are (v. 8). Such qualifications, in context, point to official responsibility.

Finally, why would Paul list qualifications for deacons' wives but not for elders' wives? It isn't as if these two lists—one for elders, one for deacons—are found in separate biblical books, where the discrepancy might be natural. The qualification lists aren't even found in separate biblical chapters; they are inseparably joined. It makes little sense to conclude that Paul thought the wives of the church's *servants* should receive scrutiny but the wives of its *leaders* should not. As Thomas Schreiner writes,

> It would seem the character of the wives of elders would be even *more* important than the wives of deacons—and thus focusing on the wives of deacons, but not on the wives of elders, is strange. Yet if the reference is to female deacons, we have an elegant explanation for why the wives of elders aren't mentioned—for the wives of deacons aren't included

---

[6] Thomas Schreiner writes, "Some object that women serving as deacons can't be in view, since Paul refers to male deacons in 3:8–10 and then returns to that theme in 3:12–13. They think the one-verse insertion about women in 3:11 can't, therefore, refer to female deacons. But the argument is not persuasive. On either view, Paul interrupts the discussion!" (Thomas Schreiner, "Does the Bible Support Female Deacons? Yes" [The Gospel Coalition. Article available at www.tgc.org/article/bible-support-female-deacons-yes]).

either. In other words, Paul isn't referring to wives at all, but to female deacons.[7]

For these reasons it is most sensible to conclude, from 1 Timothy 3, that women may serve as deacons.

3. Phoebe Was a Deacon, Not Just a Servant

As we saw earlier, Paul begins greeting the Roman church with a specific commendation:

> I commend to you our sister Phoebe, a servant [*diakonos*] of the church at Cenchreae, that you may welcome her in the Lord in a way worthy of the saints, and help her in whatever she may need from you, for she has been a patron of many and of myself as well. (Rom. 16:1–2)

Though many interpret *diakonos* informally (e.g., a servant-hearted person), there are better reasons to believe that the word signals the formal position of deacon.

First, the ending of the word is masculine, not feminine. This would have been an odd way for Paul to refer to a woman—unless, of course, he's not describing her character but designating her office.[8]

---

[7] Schreiner, "Does the Bible Support Female Deacons? Yes."

[8] In an article titled "Did the Apostles Establish the Office of Deaconess?" church historian Michael Svigel explains, "Whenever the Greek phrase '_____ of the church' is used in the New Testament and the earliest Christian literature (where '_____' is a personal designation or title), *the personal designation refers to an office, not just a generic function* (Acts 20:17; Eph. 5:23; Jas. 5:14; Rev. 2:1, 8, 12, 18; 3:1, 7, 14; Ignatius, *Trallians* 2.3; *Philadelphians* 5.1; *Polycarp* 1.1; *Shepherd of Hermas*, Vision 2.2.6; 2.4.3; 3.9.7; *Martyrdom of Polycarp* 16.2; 19.2). Therefore, if Phoebe is merely a 'helpful assistant' of the church at Cenchreae in Romans 16:1, this is the only time the construction is used this way in the earliest Christian literature." Available at http://www.retrochristianity.org/2012/04/14/did-the-apostles-establish-the-office-of-deaconess.

Second, it is significant that Phoebe is called a *diakonos* of a specific church. Throughout the New Testament this term is often used in a general sense—and rightly translated "servant" or "minister"—since the person's labor isn't tied to a specific locale, much less to a specific church. Thus Paul is a *diakonos* "of the gospel" (Eph. 3:7), Epaphras "of Christ" (Col. 1:7), Tychicus "in the Lord" (Eph. 6:21), and Timothy "of Christ Jesus" (1 Tim. 4:6). On first glance it might seem Paul is placing Phoebe into this same "general servant" category, but this overlooks that he describes her as a *diakonos* "of the church at Cenchreae," specifying her function as *diakonos* to that specific church.

This one-church designation is even more striking when we consider the expansiveness of Phoebe's ministry: she belongs to the church in Cenchreae; she is serving Paul in Corinth; and she will likely carry the letter to Rome. Yet despite this service to churches across the Roman Empire, Paul tethers her *diakonos* status to a single congregation. The most natural conclusion, then, is that "*diakonos* of the church at Cenchreae" is not a general description but an official title. There are countless general servants of *the* church, but Phoebe is also a formal deacon of *a* church.

Finally, Phoebe is called a "patron" (ESV) or "benefactor" (NIV) in verse 2, indicating that she regularly supported, perhaps financially, those in need. This task, as well as serving as a courier or envoy to Rome, would fit naturally with a diaconal position.

DEACONESSES IN CHURCH HISTORY

The presence of women deacons or deaconesses throughout Christian history has not been uniform, nor always even common. Nevertheless, they have always existed in the church, and so the practice cannot fairly be dismissed as a recent trend.

Here is a historical sampling.[9]

Pliny the Younger, Governor of Bithynia, Letter to the Emperor Trajan (AD 111–113):

Accordingly, I judged it all the more necessary to find out what the truth was by torturing two female slaves who were called deaconesses. But I discovered nothing else but depraved, excessive superstition.[10]

Clement of Alexandria (AD 150–215):

We are also aware of all the things that the noble Paul prescribed on the subject of female deacons in one of the two Epistles to Timothy.[11]

Origen of Alexandria (AD 184–253):

[Romans 16:1] teaches . . . two things: that there are . . . women deacons in the church, and that women, who have given assistance to so many people and who by their good works deserve to be praised by the apostle, ought to be accepted in the diaconate.[12]

Olympias (AD 368–408):

Olympias, a widowed deaconess of the church in Constantinople, leveraged her immense wealth to become a generous patron of

---

[9] Several of these quotations can be found in J. A. Medders's article "Why Have Women Deacons?" and David Schrock's handout "Getting Our Deacons in a Row: Lessons from Church History (the Early Church)." Available, respectively, at https://jamedders.com/why-have-women-deacons, and at https://viaemmaus.files.wordpress.com/2019/06/getting-our-deacons-in-a-row_church-history1_early-church.pdf.

[10] Pliny the Younger, *Letters* 10.96.

[11] Clement, *Commentary on 1 Corinthians* 9:5; *Stromata* 3, 6, 53.3–4.

[12] Origen, *Commentary on Romans*, 10:17, quoted in Roger Gryson, *The Ministry of Women in the Early Church* (Collegeville, MN: Liturgical Press, 1976), 136.

the church. She donated many of her estates to the church, supported the ministries of such church leaders as John Chrysostom and Gregory of Nazianzus, ransomed exiled captives, sustained a community of 250 virgins, and cared for the poor.[13]

Apostolic Constitutions (AD 380):

Ordain also a deaconess who is faithful and holy, for the ministrations toward women. For sometimes he cannot send a deacon, who is a man, to the women, on account of unbelievers. Thou shalt therefore send a woman, a deaconess, on account of the imaginations of the bad. For we stand in need of a woman, a deaconess, for many necessities.[14]

Let the deacons be in all things unspotted, as the bishop himself is to be, only more active; in number according to the largeness of the church, that they may minister to the infirm as workmen that are not ashamed. *And let the deaconess be diligent in taking care of the women*; but both of them ready to carry messages, to travel about, to minister, and to serve. . . . Let every one therefore know his proper place, and discharge it diligently with one consent, with one mind, as knowing the reward of their ministration.[15]

O Eternal God, the Father of our Lord Jesus Christ, the Creator of man and of woman, who didst replenish with the Spirit Miriam, and Deborah, and Anna, and Huldah; who didst not disdain that thy only begotten Son should be born of a woman; who also in the tabernacle of the testimony, and in the temple, didst ordain

---

[13] Gregg R. Allison, *Historical Theology: An Introduction to Christian Doctrine* (Grand Rapids, MI: Zondervan Academic, 2011), 25–26.

[14] Quoted in Allison, *Historical Theology*, 431.

[15] "Constitutions of the Holy Apostles," in *Fathers of the Third and Fourth Centuries: Lactantius, Venantius, Asterius, Victorinus, Dionysius, Apostolic Teaching and Constitutions, Homily, and Liturgies*, in *The Ante-Nicene Fathers*, ed. Alexander Roberts, James Donaldson, and A. Cleveland Coxe, trans. James Donaldson, vol. 7 (New York: Christian Literature Company, 1886), 432.

women to be keepers of thy holy gates—do thou now also look down upon this thy servant, *who is to be ordained to the office of a deaconess*, and grant her thy Holy Spirit, and "cleanse her from all filthiness of flesh and spirit," that she may worthily discharge the work which is committed to her to thy glory, and the praise of thy Christ, with whom glory and adoration be to thee and the Holy Spirit forever. Amen.[16]

John Chrysostom (AD 349–407):

Some have thought that [1 Tim. 3:11] is said of women generally, but it is not so, for why should [Paul] introduce anything about women to interfere with his subject? He is speaking of those who hold the rank of deaconesses.[17]

Jerome (AD 347–420):

Salvina, however, consecrated her life to deeds of piety, and became one of Chrysostom's deaconesses.[18]

John Calvin (1509–1564):

Deaconesses were appointed, not to soothe God by chantings or unintelligible murmurs, and spend the rest of their time in idleness, but to perform a public ministry of the church toward the poor, and to labor with all zeal, assiduity, and diligence, in offices of charity.[19]

---

[16] "Constitutions of the Holy Apostles," 492.

[17] John Chrysostom, "Homilies of St. John Chrysostom, Archbishop of Constantinople, on the First Epistle of St. Paul the Apostle to Timothy," in *Saint Chrysostom: Homilies on Galatians, Ephesians, Philippians, Colossians, Thessalonians, Timothy, Titus, and Philemon*, in *A Select Library of the Nicene and Post-Nicene Fathers of the Christian Church*, First Series, ed. Philip Schaff, trans. James Tweed and Philip Schaff, vol. 13 (New York: Christian Literature Company, 1889), 441.

[18] Jerome, "The Letters of St. Jerome," in *St. Jerome: Letters and Select Works*, in *A Select Library of the Nicene and Post-Nicene Fathers of the Christian Church*, Second Series, ed. Philip Schaff and Henry Wace, trans. W. H. Fremantle, G. Lewis, and W. G. Martley, vol. 6 (New York: Christian Literature Company, 1893), 163.

[19] John Calvin, *Institutes of the Christian Religion*, vol. 4, ch. 13, sect. 19, trans. Henry Beveridge (Peabody, MA: Hendrickson, 2008), 840.

Charles Spurgeon (1834–1892):

> Deaconesses, an office that most certainly was recognised in the apostolic churches.[20]

> It would be a great mercy if God gave us the privilege of having many sons who all preached the gospel, and many daughters who were all eminent in the church as teachers, deaconesses, missionaries, and the like.[21]

RICH BLESSING TO THE CHURCH

As we have seen, strong arguments exist on both sides of this issue. My personal persuasion after much consideration is that the office of deacon, when properly understood in Scripture, is indeed open to qualified women. I believe this is God's good intention, designed for the flourishing of everyone—women *and* men—within the household of faith, and I think that churches who close the diaconal office to qualified sisters are, however unwittingly, impoverishing themselves.

Nevertheless, I do not wish to be dogmatic in this view, and I certainly respect the many godly believers who disagree with me. As we await that time of eternal clarity "when the perfect comes [and] the partial will pass away" (1 Cor. 13:10), there is room for both conclusions in the kingdom of God.

---

[20] C. H. Spurgeon, *The Metropolitan Tabernacle Pulpit Sermons*, vol. 13 (London: Passmore & Alabaster, 1867), 589.
[21] C. H. Spurgeon, *The Metropolitan Tabernacle Pulpit Sermons*, vol. 51 (London: Passmore & Alabaster, 1905), 259.

Appendix 2

SAMPLE QUESTIONS FOR DEACON CANDIDATES

Our church's elders ask every prospective deacon to complete the following questionnaire.

———

Thank you very much for taking the time to answer these questions! It will greatly help us in thinking through who should serve our church as deacons. Because deacons are one of only two church "offices" described in Scripture, we take our deacon positions very seriously and want them to function well for the good of the church. So thanks again for your help in making that happen.

1. How long have you been a Christian? Give a brief account of your conversion.

2. Do you desire to be a deacon?

3. Do you think you have the experience and skills necessary to do the work for which the elders are considering nominating you?

4. If you are married, what does your spouse think about you serving as a deacon?

5. In what areas of service have you been involved in the life of the church?

6. Looking at 1 Timothy 3:8–13, do you think you meet the qualifications Paul lays out there for deacons?

7. Are you dignified? What do you think that means?

8. Are you double-tongued? What do you think that means?

9. Do you think you're marked by greed?

10. Do you "hold the mystery of the faith with a clear conscience"? In other words, do you sincerely and solidly believe in Jesus Christ as your Lord and Savior?

11. Do you think you've been tested in the life of the church? How? How do you think the "test" has gone?

12. Do you have a tendency to slander others, to speak ill of them in private, to gossip?

13. Are you sober-minded, able to "keep your head" in difficult situations? One of the most important roles of deacons

is to be "shock absorbers" in the life of the church. Can you do that well?

14. Are you faithful? Are you able to take responsibility for things and get them done in a timely fashion? How much of a procrastinator are you?

15. If you're married, how do you think you're doing in your role as husband/wife? As father/mother?

16. Read 1 Timothy 3:13. What do you think it will mean in your particular situation to "serve well as a deacon"? How do you think serving well as a deacon will increase your confidence in the faith that is in Christ Jesus?

17. Do you use social media of any kind (Twitter, Facebook, etc.)? How do you think Paul's description of a deacon applies to how a deacon, in particular, should engage social media?

18. Have you read our church constitution? Do you have any questions about the way our church functions? Will you be happy to abide by that constitution and defend and explain it to other members when necessary?

GENERAL INDEX

SCRIPTURE INDEX

IX 9Marks

Building Healthy Churches

9Marks exists to equip church leaders with a biblical vision and practical resources for displaying God's glory to the nations through healthy churches.

To that end, we want to see churches characterized by these nine marks of health:

1. Expositional Preaching
2. Gospel Doctrine
3. A Biblical Understanding of Conversion and Evangelism
4. Biblical Church Membership
5. Biblical Church Discipline
6. A Biblical Concern for Discipleship and Growth
7. Biblical Church Leadership
8. A Biblical Understanding of the Practice of Prayer
9. A Biblical Understanding and Practice of Missions

Find all our Crossway titles and other resources at 9Marks.org.

9MARKS: BUILDING HEALTHY CHURCHES SERIES

Based on Mark Dever's best-selling book *Nine Marks of a Healthy Church*, each book in this series helps readers grasp basic biblical commands regarding the local church.

TITLES INCLUDE:

Biblical Theology	Corporate Worship	The Gospel
Church Discipline	Deacons	Missions
Church Elders	Discipling	Prayer
Church Membership	Evangelism	Sound Doctrine
Conversion	Expositional Preaching	

For more information, visit crossway.org.
For translated versions of these and other 9Marks books, visit 9Marks.org/bookstore/translations.